EDUCATION—THE LOST DIMENSION

Education—

THE

LOST DIMENSION

W. R. NIBLETT

with a Foreword by Margaret Mead

William Sloane Associates, Inc., New York, 1955

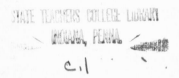

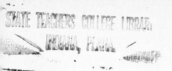
CONTENTS

ACKNOWLEDGEMENTS

I am grateful to Dr. Margaret Mead and her publishers, William Morrow and Co., of New York, for permission to quote a passage from *Growing Up in New Guinea;* and to Mr. A. R. Bielby and the University of Leeds Institute of Education for allowing me to draw upon his paper on General Education in the Sixth Form, published in the *Researches and Studies* of that Institute; and to T. S. Eliot and Harcourt, Brace and Company, Inc., for permission to quote from *The Cocktail Party* and *Family Reunion.*

W. R. N.

Leeds, 1955

FOREWORD

This is a book for those who are interested either as parents or teachers in the cultivation of personality in children and young people. The author is one of those rare moderns who can say both that science is here to stay and that science is not enough, who can discuss with competence and respect the great strength of cultural traditions and insist that there is still room for the unexpected contribution of each individual spirit. Far from encouraging pessimism or despair, the book evokes in the reader a desire to find someone to teach at once, to seek for an imagination to cherish, a sensitivity to protect.

Professor Niblett lays particular stress on the responsibility of the teacher to recognize the diverse cultural and temperamental strands which are combined in one personality so that he may emphasize some, damp down others. His emphasis is particularly pertinent today when we are re-examining such fundamentals of our educational philosophy as the place of discipline, the meaning of privacy, and the importance of a knowledge of suffering and grief for a fuller comprehension of human experience. Whereas so many writers, either out of a faith in religious education or a reliance on the great books of the past for forming the character of the present generation, end up with a complete neglect of the revolution which has taken place in our conception of character—due to the developments in psychology and anthropology—the author makes no such error. Religious belief, the right to wonder, the sense of mystery are seen as fulfillment for the individual in any age and not as dogmatically asserted imperatives which would negate all that we have learned about Man in the last fifty years. The book does not advocate going back to anything, but rather insists on going forward in an age made difficult by the moral imperatives of science to preserve a disciplined tentativeness.

This little book, written from England, relevant for all the English-speaking peoples of the world, has also a peculiar relevance to the problem we face, in that we have attempted to turn professions requiring dedication into merely well-paid jobs. In the United States, as in many other parts of the world, the professions which are primarily concerned with teaching, cherishing, and caring for human beings have a dual, and partly contradictory, place in society. Men and women enter the professions of teaching, medicine, the ministry, social work, nursing, because their imaginations are caught by opportunities to work with and minister to other human beings. But they also enter them as ways of improving their social status, a way of climbing in one generation out of a very simple background into a respected position in the community. Added to this, American society has been desperately careless and exploitative of that rare and essential ingredient of dedication—an enthusiastic, spontaneous delight in working with and for other people, rather than in working with things, for money or power, or even in working as the artist or the scientist works, for the sheer joy of the working, "each in his separate star." We have tended to leave the most exactingly personal of tasks, elementary teaching, nursing, case work, to women, and we have paid them very, very badly—so badly that vast groups of women have had to leave the profession of their choice in order to support those dependents whom they, especially the unmarried women, so frequently have. Looking at a situation in which there are no longer enough teachers or nurses or skilled social workers, we have concluded that this is so because they are so poorly paid. We have raised the pay and thereby permitted some of those to continue who would have been forced to leave their calling —a lovely word too little used today—but at the same time we now fail to attract those with a calling.

We rely on the appeals of good salary and professional status to attract recruits into these fields of dedication—and with horrid results. Aspiring young students give as their reasons for choosing one of these professions: salary, congenial work, short hours, long vacations. In the resulting clamor, the only motives which can keep a teacher genuinely happy in the hot and chalky smell of the crowded schoolroom on a rainy day, in the day-by-day patient zippering up of nursery leggings, get badly neglected. We greatly need to re-emphasize that all of these things—salary, hours, status, working conditions—are merely ways which enable those who want to teach, to teach, but never adequate reasons in themselves for becoming a teacher.

Professor Niblett lays a great deal of sensitive stress on learning to learn; on all the unspoken, even unmeant, communication which goes on from adult to child, from one child to another; on the importance of atmosphere. His own book performs this service which he describes so eloquently —it communicates an excitement about the essential possibilities of teaching. For all those who have found delight in teaching or in being taught, it states with the vigor and freshness in which we love to greet our deepest aspirations what an extraordinary privilege it is to educate—even a single child.

MARGARET MEAD

New York, June 24, 1955

1

DIRECTION OF TRAVEL

1

Many people throughout the West assume that the real business of living is the achievement of prosperity and "happiness." That assumption must be challenged for two reasons. For one thing, it cannot be true—it leaves out a whole dimension of human experience; for another, though it may breed a superficial activity, it breeds also an inward listlessness, a sense, widespread in our generation, that there is little permanent significance or import in life. Much activity today, even quite desirable activity, brings satisfaction only while it is in progress. When it is past, there is a blank, and we hurry to fill the vacuum with more action. Education itself, once the infant stage is over and it has begun in earnest, is apt tacitly to assume that its proper function is to help children—and indeed whole nations—to "get on," so that more money, more power, and therefore more happiness will eventually be theirs.

It is not difficult to understand the argument or the desires that lie behind it. But there are signs that a creed of "getting on" is failing to satisfy at any depth many of those who hold it. What are comfort and leisure for when we have attained them? Perhaps, after all, men were better off when they could feel quietly sure that faith and vision were the birthright of mankind, even if individually they could not all be its vehicles. To numbers of people in the seventeenth century, for example, moments of insight were more normal and natural than they are now.

> "The Heavens were an oracle and spake
>   Divinity: the Earth did undertake
>   The office of a priest; and I being dumb—
>   (Nothing besides was dumb)—all things did come
>   With voices and instructions." [1]

We no longer hear such voices and life has certainly lost in meaning as a consequence. We can hardly believe today even in progress.

It is not to be expected that a satisfying philosophy of education will be widely spread when a satisfying philosophy of life is so seldom achieved. If life lacks a sense of direction, so will the education it is possible to give our children whether at home or in school. A generous allowance of pocket money with which to purchase ice cream and happiness may well be an unconscious confession of inability to impart gifts more valuable. In a time such as ours of holiday from conviction some kinds of learning

[1] Thomas Traherne: *Dumbness.*

will not take place at all and our young people will be left, as many are left today, on the loose. Even techniques and skills themselves—looking, listening, reading, writing—will be acquired with less effectiveness and less intensity. And to try to meet the challenge, as we may be tempted to do, with a reply in material terms is not to meet it: no multiplication—however desirable in itself—in the number of new schools and laboratories, of youth centres or technical colleges, will answer such questions; no re-arrangement of secondary education so that more of it is transferred from high schools to junior colleges; no piercing of still more entrances into our universities.

What has brought about this state of affairs? What can be done to remedy it?

Among the causes of our lack of purpose and direction, no doubt, are two major wars in forty years, the great depression of the Thirties and a gnawing anxiety about the insecure state of the world, the fragile balance of forces within it. But the failure of nerve threatened even in the first decade of the century and is not, I fancy, unconnected with one of man's greatest achievements—the gradual spread of the scientific temper. A scientific temper must necessarily encourage detachment; it must incline men to concentrate on objective phenomena as being the best fitted for steady observation, controllable experiment and useful discovery.

But an analytic habit of mind, of untold promise as an instrument, has its dangers. Because we are looking for truth through microscopes and testing it by logical processes of examination and reasoning it will be easy to be prevented from seeing much that is true. "We have inherited a naive faith in the substantiality and ultimacy of facts," says Susanne K. Langer, "and are convinced that human life, to have any value, must be not only casually and opportunely adapted to their exigencies (as even the most other-worldly lives have been), but must be intellectually filled with an appreciation of 'things as they are.' Facts are our very measure of value."[2] We owe an immense debt to science, and the future of mankind must more and more be influenced by its findings and applications, but Samuel Butler's subtle fears that we might become its slaves—though in deeper ways than the Erewhonians—ought still to be arrows in our conscience.

As long as science was content to deal with the apparently objective world it was possible, of course, to remain as untroubled by its findings as were most of the early Victorians. Chemistry, geology, even physics, dealt—however analytically—with matter and things comfortably separate from man. But the publication of *The Origin of Species* in 1859 showed to the many that science could disturbingly include within its province both the animal and the human; and by the end of the nineteenth century it was clear that the human mind itself, the very springs and hidden motives of action, could also be subjected to analysis. We were no longer safe. If our actions were the products of instinctive drives, of conflicts and 'compensations,' were we not, after all, as the behaviourists began to whisper, merely mechanisms functioning in an extraordinarily complex way? By the middle of the twentieth century the sociologists seem to be demonstrating clearly that

[2] *Philosophy in a New Key*. Mentor Edition, p. 221. For complete listing of titles quoted or referred to, see Bibliography.

we are all patterned and largely determined by the social groups to which we belong, that the laws of social development are as inexorable as the laws of chemical change. What is the use then of pretending any longer to believe in the freedom of man, or of supposing that in reality all men are not prisoners in the universe?

Scientific method is the product of high intelligence rigorously applied. And such honour do we pay—quite rightly —to the men who seem to be heroically following Truth wherever she may lead, that even if we half refuse to credit the findings or theories of economists, psychologists, sociologists, even physicists, we are very likely to be driven in doing so into the 'uninvolved' mood that is common today the world over. "The experts may soon have a different theory to put forward to account for this or that. So don't let us commit ourselves deeply to any of them or to anything. Let us be, like the scientists themselves, as detached as we can; and just wait." Such a mood must regard enthusiasm, vision and commitment with a cynical eye: the best that men can do is to state their own doubts and uncertainties honestly and plainly; and learn to endure.

Nor is this all. Our historical situation being what it is, many men and women even of serious mind wonder whether faith and a sense of purpose, even if we had them, would any longer be of much use. For the hydrogen bomb is waiting ready to hand and, given an intense enough moment of impatience and despair, what is there to prevent its being dropped, to bring sudden and untold catastrophe with it? Can one see ahead steadily or far in days such as ours? Of what use then is hope—or confidence? Are they not themselves deceiving sentimentalities?

And yet, as we know deep in the heart, we need them if life is to be lived and not merely endured, or, in one ingenious way or another, escaped from. For without them there is no future. To have beliefs and a sense of purpose is to live in harmony with the nature of things. To wish to escape for long from purposes and loves and commitments is like wanting to escape outside an atmosphere of air.

Our second question remains: what can be done to educate men so that they will be able to live with more depth, to be less escapist? In such times as ours it is tempting to underestimate the importance in life of imagination, of a heart "that watches and receives," of a human understanding of other people. To do so is to dam the flow of spiritual energy near its source. In a world dominated by technical achievements it is easy to be shallow. To the question: "What can man accomplish in life?" the superficial, but common, answer is, "He can achieve as much as his technologies will let him."

But through awe and pity and love men can find out truths they will never discover with a brain working on its own, intellectually. The study of human capacities and human motives by psychologists and physiologists, whether the emphasis is upon measurement or dynamics, can easily persuade the young that there is, after all, little mystery about man and human life. Experiment, however, can never be a substitute for experiencing and analysis at no time a substitute for mystery. There is great need today for children to be brought into touch with the greater than man. They need an education that has a religious quality in it: and the first thing about religious education is not that doctrines should be taught but that worship should be made possible.

If indeed we are to survive the winds blowing so strongly and so coldly through our time, there is a need for roots. Roots must be grown before any flower can blossom. Some of our roots are the traditions which helped the West itself in days past to grow into a civilization. Its dependence upon revelation, upon truths "felt along the heart," and upon religious faith, is one of the prime sources and secrets of its culture, of the poetry and science and art—and the law and the music too—which have been among its greatest gifts to the world.

2

In this book we shall first try to face some elemental facts about the nature of education. Every child is immensely affected by the society in which he is brought up, but he takes for granted the habits and customs and the evaluations of that society. We are apt to underestimate greatly the subtlety and unconsciousness of much of the educative process, the extent to which it is the product of forces within society generally, and because of this we tend to identify it too much with what goes on in schools. Schools, indispensable in any modern state, are by no means necessarily the most powerful educative factors in the lives of those who attend them; though it is true that a school which is moribund can hinder some very vital kinds of learning or even make them impossible, and equally true that one which is vital can awaken talent which would otherwise have perished. In the history of education, some homes and schools—it is a point not often enough noticed —have undoubtedly been as good at killing off musical or mathematical ability or even effective intelligence itself as others have been successful in bringing them to life and light. A great deal of fundamental education, whether received outside school or within it, must have the character of indoctrination, though the doctrines will by no means be passed on at a conscious level.

Secondly, we shall contend that "society" is an unreal abstraction considered apart from the individual human beings, past, present and to come, who make it up. Its views, its fears and its hopes exist because individuals hold them and believe in them. But in any society a great complexity of strands, of subtly differing views and ideals, are held together. The same is true of the individual himself: he too binds together in one more or less unified personality many divergent and inconsistent ideals, tendencies and opinions. A society is open to modification and change in temper by those alive within it, and most effectively by those who belong to it centrally and securely and yet hold new and slightly different views from the ones dominantly accepted. Because society is so complex, it is even possible for some of its traditions to become buried (and so "recessive") within it; some individuals are brought up with very different traditions emphasized (or "dominant") in their education from those given prime place in the upbringing of others living in the same community. Now men may have much more to contribute to the needs of the next half-century if certain tendencies within them are strongly developed than if the chief stimulus is given to the growth of others. If we can be detached enough, we can indeed see for ourselves in the face of many a young child potentialities which might have been developed in one society but in another will not be: potentialities for saintliness maybe or, on the other hand, for lust, for kindliness or for a cold lack of human sympathy.

Which potentialities are in fact developed will depend to some extent upon the traditions of the society concerned. A number of characteristics which might have been developed in a man may not come into functional existence because of the particular race or society or class to which he belongs. Today education, in so far as it is under our control, must be especially concerned about which of the variants within the main traditions of our society shall be allowed greater scope in those we educate. In the past we have been less conscious of the selective processes we employed in our schools—through control of 'atmosphere,' choice of staff, kinds of teacher training, choice of curricula, weightings of time-table—than we need to be or, indeed, dare to be any longer.

Thirdly, we shall argue that since among the greatest needs of our time are those for new vision and a new depth of purpose in western civilization, we must recognise the importance of insight and feeling as well as thought, see the necessity for beliefs, admit that there is a place for mystery as well as knowledge in the mind of man. Education must undoubtedly be concerned with life "in the flat," that is, with the task of seeing that people learn many techniques: how to read, write, add and multiply; how to speak and behave more or less as other people do in the nation of which they are members; how to keep themselves and others healthy and sane in a world dangerous to live in and in the mid-twentieth century becoming still more dangerous. For many people no doubt this training for life in the flat comprises the whole that education needs to be concerned about. Indeed, they ask, is not this already far too much for comfort? But for others, including myself, it is not enough. Happiness and sanity are not only quantitative but qualitative: they vary not only in amount but in depth. The end of education is not "happiness" but rather to develop greater capacity for being aware; to deepen human understanding—perhaps inevitably through conflict, struggle and suffering; to awaken and discipline a true power of reason; to make right action natural.

If leadership is to be released—and there need be no lack of it—several conditions must be fulfilled. Leaders must add vision to intelligence and will, but not merely that: they must be representative of their society, belonging to it profoundly. For unless they do thus belong, they will never feel intimately as disturbingly personal issues the conflicts really important in its life, and so will never be able to fight its battles within themselves. Only an heir can carry on a succession. The problem of making a college or a university deeply representative of the nation in this sense is one which has only very partially been solved as yet either in England or America—even in Yale or Oxford, in Cambridge or Princeton.

2

GROUP INFLUENCES
AND THEIR SIGNIFICANCE

1

The study of the influence of society upon the individual has made giant strides in the past quarter of a century. The many exciting contributions made by sociology to our knowledge of human limitation, of human possibility and the mechanisms of social change, are bound to have their effects upon educational practice both inside and outside school. Indeed the findings of sociology may be as seminal in their influence upon the study and organization of education in the next fifty years as the findings of psychology were in the last fifty. For what the sociological approach has done is to bring far more openly to the light of day the permeating—and to a large extent prophesiable—effects upon the unconscious mind of living and learning in one society rather than another. In a sense, of course, we knew all this before, but at the same time we were not aware of it; we could conveniently forget and not reckon with our knowledge.

When I set foot in France, for example, I am always surprised to find that even the smallest children are talking French and not English. Of course, it is "natural" for them to speak it, just as it is natural for small English and American children to begin talking in English. But so subtle are the effects of their environment—their speech environment—upon these talkative French children, that it is not only the words they say but the very structure and intimate rhythm of their sentences that is French. The lilt, the dialect, the very nuances of the speech of their families are rapidly becoming theirs. And what is true of the acquisition of a language is true also of a dozen other learnings: of when and what we should eat, of when to smile and frown, of behaviour patterns in all their complexity, of what to notice as we go about the world, even of what "our" world is—different from the Indian world, or the Russian world, or the Japanese world because of the different presuppositions we have assimilated.

It is impossible to think of any human baby surviving for long simply as an individual. From the moment of his coming into the world he is a member of a group, in the large majority of cases of a family group, but even in the rare cases where mother and father and family are all removed at a very early hour, still a member of a group of nurses, friends or foster parents who look after him. The immense influence of the group or society upon the individual who belongs to it is more easily seen when we consider some more primitive society than our own and see these influences actually at work.

Compare, for example, the upbringing of a Manus baby as described in Margaret Mead's *Growing up in New Guinea* with the sort of treatment which a typical English or American baby will get. The Manus people live in lagoon villages in pile houses standing like long-legged birds out of the water.

"The Manus baby is accustomed to water from the first years of his life. Lying on the slatted floor he watches the sunlight gleam on the surface of the lagoon as the changing tide passes and repasses beneath the house. . . . When he is about a year old, he has learned to grasp his mother firmly about the throat, so that he can ride in safety, poised on the back of her neck. She has carried him up and down the long house, dodged under low-hanging shelves, and climbed up and down the rickety ladders which lead from house floor down to the landing verandah. The decisive, angry gesture with which he was reseated on his mother's neck whenever his grip tended to slacken has taught him to be alert and sure-handed. At last it is safe for his mother to take him out in a canoe, to punt or paddle the canoe herself while the baby clings to her neck. If a sudden wind roughens the lagoon or her punt catches in a rock, the canoe may swerve and precipitate mother and baby into the sea. The water is cold and dark, acrid in taste and blindingly salt; the descent into its depths is sudden, but the training within the house holds good. The baby does not loosen his grip while his mother rights the canoe and climbs out of the water. . . .

"Understanding canoe and sea come just a little later than the understanding of house and fire, which form part of the child's environment from birth. A child's knowledge of a canoe is considered adequate if he can balance himself, feet planted on the two narrow rims, and punt the canoe with accuracy, paddle well enough to steer through a mild gale, run the canoe accurately under a house without jamming the outrigger, extricate a canoe from a flotilla of canoes crowded closely about a house platform or the edge of an islet, and bail out a canoe by a deft backward and forward movement which dips the bow and stern alternately. It does not include any sailing knowledge. Understanding of the sea includes swimming, diving, swimming under water, and a knowledge of how to get water out of the nose and throat by leaning the head forward and striking the back of the neck. Children of between five and six have mastered these four necessary departments." [1]

The sort of education received by these South Sea Island babies is alarmingly different from the sort which English or American children get in their homes and their nursery schools and kindergartens. All the time environment is taken for granted, yet it is precisely the environment which matters so much and so subtly. The adaptability and flexibility of human nature is beyond all telling, especially in early years. No one knows the limits of possibility for it. The Manus children described in the passages quoted were learning how to use their physical powers according to certain laws and patterns of achievement made for them by the habits of their race. They were inheritors of a tradition which their parents and all their relatives simply took for granted.

Away in the cold north, Eskimos live cosy and warm within their furs and their igloos. But not merely that. Most of them, like most other people in the world, live for

[1] *Growing Up in New Guinea,* Mentor Edition, pp. 23, 30. Also available in the omnibus edition—*From the South Seas: Studies of Adolescence and Sex in Primitive Societies,* Morrow, New York, 1939.

most of their time cosy and warm in the spirit within their own society and its traditions. It was an Eskimo chieftain who remarked, "We observe our ancient customs so that the universe may be preserved." Every group of people is bound and fastened together by its customs and faith and by the ways of feeling and thinking common within it.

Birth is the beginning of men's lives as individuals in the world; but it is not really the start of their way of life on earth, for that took place ages ago in the dim pre-historical past. They are all of them brought up, as it were, to obey the secret laws, important or unimportant, of their own social group or groups, hardly knowing that they obey them. Schools of every type tend to take for granted and teach an outlook and behaviour acceptable to the so-cial group they represent. They are not free to teach even speech habits more than a little different from those which the parents of their children wish them to have. Undoubt-edly the parents must have approved when at one well-known English school for girls, about 1815, maidens were taught among other things "to use a pocket handkerchief with delicacy" and "to faint gracefully upon any sudden disaster, or at the theatre when a despairing lover stabbed himself."

The authority of custom and tradition is extraordinarily powerful and permeating. "For once that a deep convic-tion is the parent of a habit," as Coleridge said, "a habit is a hundred times the parent of a conviction." [2] Even the most civilized Greeks in the time of Plato, including Plato himself, accepted the naturalness and inevitability of slav-ery. In the Middle Ages and in Elizabethan times in Eng-

[2] MS. note, quoted in Coburn: *Inquiring Spirit*, p. 80.

land it was extremely difficult not to believe in witches —as indeed it was for many citizens in Salem, Mass., in the late seventeenth century. This was no matter of intelligence or lack of brains, for the average intelligence even of our medieval ancestors was probably as high as ours. In the West, our respect for the law is the result of a long and painful experience and history. Our manners and our behaviour would seem odd to a South Sea Islander: but *we* may find it natural enough to raise our hats; to stand at attention as we sing the national anthem; to cheer at football games but to remain silent in railroad cars. The rhythms of our speech are the results of an imitation so unconscious that it is only with a real effort that we notice our own accent or our peculiar way of using a word. The authority of traditions and custom is a strong authority: it takes unusual individuality to challenge it. Brought up in a primitive society we should be primitive; brought up in a Communist society most of us would be Communists.

A child of a President of the United States, or of an Archbishop, reared in a jungle by the folk of the jungle, would develop into a heathen child, nasty and brutish even if tall. Education, in the essential sense of education to fit into the cultural pattern of the surrounding society, begins at birth if not before it.[3] At no stage in the growth of the human individual to maturity is the considerable educative importance of group influences, often largely unconscious in their operation, to be gainsaid. But in the early months and years they are the *chief* educative influences. It is simply not possible to remain a nationally unbiased baby for long or to remain unbiased, as it were, by

[3] Cf. Ralph Linton, *The Cultural Background of Personality*, pp. 27-54.

the period into which one has been born. To start with
there is extremely little to differentiate an early thirteenth-
century baby from a mid-twentieth-century one, or many
a baby born in Middlesex or Wyoming from many a baby
born in the Ukraine. But all kinds of loyalties quickly begin to grow—loyalties to family, to language, to locality, to
school, to form, to team.

For most children in England or America, or any country, the home is the most powerful educative group they
will ever encounter. Speaking generally, it is in the home
that the life of the child begins to develop and come to
flower. It is his *intimate* environment. The home gives the
child a freedom that is more absolute in quality than he
will get anywhere else. In it, he is given from babyhood a
greater chance of really feeling and expressing himself
without having to consider the consequences than he can
be given in any more public institution. He finds in the
home an environment of affection and regard in which
growth is a natural thing.

In a good home, his physical well-being is encouraged
by the food and drink, air and exercise available for him.
But the mother and home nourish his mental and emotional development by providing him with a background
of absolute trust and by taking a warm interest in his doings and his questions. Nothing he can do in his younger
years can alienate him or make him not, in essentials, still
one of the family. The home is very largely responsible
for the development of the young child's emotional health
as well as his physical health; for it is in the home that he
gets so many of the emotional experiences which matter so
much to his development. And much has been written in

recent years to show the devastating results of the failure of the home to accept this responsibility.

Power to love and to trust are affected by the home—not so much by what is said or even done in it as by the outlook and expectations that are current. The intensity, depth, and subtlety of this part of the educative process are still far from being adequately realized: we are indeed only at the beginning of our knowledge of the intricate ways in which it is important. A child, particularly a young child, is sensitive to and disciplined by all sorts of inhibitions and fears and affections and predilections passed on to him by his mother and by those within the circle of people accepted by the family. One has often been told how the fear of cows can be got from a companion walking with a child across a field even though nothing may be said and no evasive action of any sort taken. Still subtler transferences than that—of habit and bias, of love and loyalty—occur every day in every home.

Even our expectations themselves must be learned: a mind is dyed the colour of what it expects. When Alice fell down the rabbit hole she expected life in Wonderland to be like the life she knew. But the longer she lived in Wonderland the less she came to expect her days there to be "normal," and the more she expected life to be topsy-turvy and unprophesiable. We are not born with a particular set of expectations: they are given us by society.

In our own age we are becoming increasingly aware of the power of society over the individual. As T. S. Eliot makes the central character in his *Cocktail Party* say:

"it is often the case that my patients
Are only pieces of a total situation

Which I have to explore. The single patient
Who is ill by himself, is rather the exception."

Group influences can be immensely potent from earliest
infancy and perhaps even before it begins. Any combination of factors which places a child or an adult in a secure
and dominant position will tend to make easy the development in him of certain basic attitudes; any combination
which exposes him to insecurity will lead to the development of others. The child or the adult who feels himself an
underdog will tend either to behave in a wobbly way in
many situations or to compensate by bravado for his feelings of inferiority. It is often the unloved child who develops the most acute feelings of inferiority of all and, in
some cases, tendencies to delinquency in compensation. If
children grow up within situations which give them a fundamental trust or hope, or a strong faith in the future, they
will become (quite soberly speaking) very different people from those they would have been had they been nourished in less sunny places and a more biting air.

At home or at school much of the child's education is a
process of growing into fuller and deeper membership in
the society and civilization of which the school and the
home are in great measure products themselves. Much indeed of the education of men is made possible or quite
impossible simply by environment. The most direct means
of modifying their education will often be direct and com-
pulsory modification of that environment. But though a
change of physical surroundings will have its effects, a
change of moral atmosphere and temper will have many
more. Families are potent educationally because of the
depth to which they can reach down into affections and

loyalties and actually create "outlook" and character. It is difficult to be energetic and hard-working in a society which values and approves of laziness, to be creative and enterprising in a society which most of all has faith in the *status quo.*

In schools, what we try to teach children is determined partly by what it is physically and psychologically possible to teach them, partly by what we are able to afford to pay for them to be taught, but in great measure by what it is possible for them to be taught at that time in history. The curriculum is what it is, not because anyone sat down yesterday and planned it, but because it has grown to be like that. Neither Latin nor algebra might be thought of by a present-day planner of a school curriculum fresh to the job. And even the apparently revolutionary school is far more determined by precedent, whether it follows the precedent or reacts to it, than it likes to imagine. If teachers wanted to introduce a ruling that no more punishments should be given, to prune the time-table allowance for English to one period a fortnight, or to devote a period a week to atheistic theory, they would find it extraordinarily difficult to do so. Society itself, in the shape of parents, employers, assistant masters and mistresses, and even the pupils themselves, would see to that.

But it is not only through the curriculum that tradition imposes its authority upon education. Its impositions are more far-reaching and inward. The very type of character we wish to develop in children is influenced by the cultural pattern of which we are ourselves parts. In England and America, for instance, we think of fair play as a virtue; we admire activity, but only respect passiveness; under the impact of Christianity we acknowledge—though not always with ease—that capacity to forgive is a strength rather than a weakness. It is a mistake to think that children come into the world with personalities formed in the bud and ready to blossom with the mere passage of time. All children have to be given a great part of their character before they can develop it, and society has many subtle ways of giving people the characters which come to be theirs. It is a pure assumption that if you leave people to themselves they will develop the characters they do in fact develop in the particular society in which they are brought up. What they become depends in large measure upon the ideals, the dominant philosophy and *raison d'être* of that society. Authority has to be heard before it can be obeyed and we do not obey authorities outside the range or direction of our listening. The proclamations of the Pope are not in a true sense heard by Protestants, any more than are the utterances of the head of the Soviet government by loyal citizens of the United States. Before any speaker or writer can really be heard he has to be listened to at the level at which it is possible to understand him.

How the individual shall look at his world is in fact to a considerable extent decided for him by his society. A man born in 1890 of sound stock, brought up in a well-to-do, Christian and affectionate home, educated at Groton and Harvard, is bound to see his world very differently from a man with the same intelligence quotient, born in 1930, brought up in an agnostic home, where as a child he was not much wanted, educated first at an elementary school and then at a small country high school which he left for good, maybe without graduating, at the age of fifteen.

Change the temper of a home, a school, a university or of any society and you change the sort of individuals within it. "It is the culture of the society around us which provides the raw material from which we make our lives. If the culture is meagre we suffer, though maybe without knowing it; if it is rich we have the chance to rise to our opportunity. Every private interest of every man and woman is served by the enrichment of the traditional stores of his civilization. The richest musical sensitivity can operate only within the equipment and standards of its tradition. It will add, perhaps importantly, to that tradition, but its achievement remains in proportion to the instruments and musical theory which the culture has provided." [4] An individual may act intelligently and purposefully within a society, but, viewed from without, the range of his choices and acts of will are limited by the set of expectations which his society has made it possible for him to have. In other words, he can only be individual in certain ways and certain directions.

2

Faced with all this evidence of the power of society over the habits and very outlook of its members, and brought sharply to realize the truth of much that has been shown, modern man may react by assuming that clearly he has no freedom; all is determined for him. And so another powerful reinforcement to his cynical detachment has been made. The further dissemination of sociological knowl-

[4] Ruth Benedict: *Patterns of Culture*, p. 181.

edge may make matters still worse. For since sociology and psychology deal in experiments, investigations, researches and "facts," they are in a sense comparatively easy subjects to teach and must become still easier. The more practised the student, the more complex the psychological and sociological patterns he will be able to discern.

It is far more difficult for him to remember, first, that in order to make scientific, sociological observations at all he is removing part of himself from the field of vision. Human feeling, sharp sorrow and delight, times of joy and suffering are not less real because we think we can explain their causes; to analyze human nature is not to dissolve or explain it away. No merely intellectual comprehension by itself is enough.

Secondly, in almost every situation which confronts a human being there are choices to be made—though it may be right to see them usually as choices between the different traditions all alive within him. To act freely cannot, it is true, mean to act without predisposing, determining factors having great influence. But some acts are more free than others. A free act is a significant act, one through which a man expresses central rather than superficial parts of himself. Perhaps indeed the educational richness and potentiality of a group tends to be proportionate to the depths within a man or woman at which he can come to belong to it and contribute to it as an individual.

Thirdly, it is well to remember that all psychology and sociology live inside some philosophy of life or *Weltanschauung*, a fact which too often passes unnoticed. Our concepts of what is "normal" or "desirable" or "evolved" or "mature" are likely to be parts of our very observations. Any philosophy (or sociology inside it) which fails to notice and to reckon with moments of individual creative vision, of insight, or of hard unselfish decision, must be seriously defective.

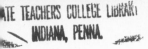

3

THE SOCIOLOGICAL APPROACH

AND ITS LIMITATIONS

1

The influence of the work of anthropologists and sociologists upon the study of education is already considerable and it is still growing. Among their most significant suggestions is the simple but far-reaching contention that if anyone is to see or understand the world around him he has to be given a point of view from which to do it. Blind people who gain their sight for the first time in adult life learn only gradually and with very great difficulty how to interpret the vision of things coming in upon them; reality and meaning continue to come in through the senses they had used hitherto because they can interpret the data those senses yield them, but as yet sight merely pours confusion upon them. Before they can see anything coherently they have to learn how to look. It is a matter of common observation that many animals do not see themselves in a mirror even when it is held right in front of them. In his close record of the development and education of the wild boy of Aveyron, who was captured in a completely savage state at the age of about twelve, Itard[1] recounts that in the early months after his capture the boy's hearing was extremely sensitive to any sound which would have been significant for him during his life in the forest, but all but entirely absent even for loud noises which would have been irrelevant to him in the wilds. Thus when a chestnut or a walnut was cracked without his knowledge and as gently as possible, he never failed to turn quickly and run towards the place from which the sound came. But human conversation near him and even the loud explosion of a shotgun in the next room were not noticed.

Before we can see, hear or even feel effectively we have to be permitted by the civilization in which we are brought up to see, hear and understand life and existence in particular ways. There are societies in which much feeling of affection for family, for brothers and sisters, or even for mother, is not permitted. Learning in what directions one's society will allow one to feel is a very primary and subtle sort of learning but nonetheless immensely important.

Another result of the sociological approach to the study of education has been to make us once again strongly aware of the power of environment. Until quite recently the tendency was to emphasize the dominant importance of heredity in the educability of men and women. But it is clear that environmental factors can be decisive in producing one kind of behaviour and attitude in one sort of society, a very different kind of attitude and conduct in another. And this, as far as it goes, is encouraging: for it is at least somewhat easier to control and modify a people's

[1] *Wild Boy of Aveyron*, pp. 26-7.

environment—even their interior mental environment—than to change their inherited characteristics.

Without any doubt, then, a sociological approach is bound to add to our realization of the scope and nature of education whether in school or outside it. What it can never do—by itself—is to give us an adequate philosophy of education. The social scientist, as a social scientist, sees human feeling and effort as contributing to a social pattern, and efficient education primarily as the process of helping people to fit into that pattern with as little waste of time and as little pain to themselves as possible. Like other scientists, he may appear to be the honest man among the self-deceivers, the one determined to face the truth. And, at first sight, it might seem that there is no defence against his contentions; for if we know the objective truth there is nothing else that can be said. But, of course, if we look at any phenomena detachedly and entirely from the outside, cause and effect, stimulus and response, are all that we shall see.

Very much of the effort of any science—biology, psychology, sociology included—is to annotate the behaviour of phenomena. There is no need for sociology or psychology or any of the sciences to *believe* in man. Indeed study of the implications of many a psychological treatise leads one to suppose that it might be better if men were content to be animals *tout simple*, untroubled by inhibition, conscience or feelings of guilt. Many psychological and sociological writings look upon men and women simply as products of social forces, urged on by their appetites to attain a variety of more or less animal "satisfactions." Throughout the Kinsey Reports, for example, runs the assumption that sexual satisfaction is one of the ultimate kinds of satisfaction and that "happiness" results from satisfaction at this level. Within the attempt of the psychoanalyst to "free" a human being, to restore him to health, to help him to regain normality, are assumptions about what normality and health and completeness are like. These assumptions themselves are products of the outlook and philosophy of life of the society in which the analyst has himself been living. Is humility a desirable, or normal, quality? or kindness? or forgiveness? The books and essays of psychologists and sociologists rarely mention them.

Every psychological or sociological theory has concealed within it various assumptions of a philosophic kind. Thus the "dynamic" school of psychologists who owe so much to Freud assume that a life free from tensions is the most desirable sort of life, that the conscious and unconscious parts of the mind will tend to become friends with each other as soon as the unconscious has been freed from all its complexes, that a social order is possible in which all men will enter into their rights. People think they will escape from the limiting human situation if they are thus freed and will overcome time. But freedom of this kind is an illusion. Man must not conceal from himself the knowledge that he is incomplete and, in this life, forever unsusceptible of completion.

For sociology as such there can be really no criteria or standards for the evaluation of conduct. Its concern is not to attribute praise or blame or to make moral judgments, but rather to record simply and calmly the pattern which has been woven. Karl Mannheim in *Ideology and Utopia* pointed out twenty years ago that increased knowledge of a sociological kind never gets rid of the need for moral decisions, but only forces them farther and farther back. "What we gain through this retreat from decisions is an expansion of our horizon and a greater intellectual mastery of our world. . . . Whenever we become aware of a determinant which has dominated us, we remove it from the realm of unconscious motivation into that of the controllable, calculable and objectified. Choice and decision are thereby not eliminated; on the contrary, motives which previously dominated us become subject to our domination; we are more and more thrown back upon our true self." [2]

There is often, nevertheless, in sociological writings a subtle unwillingness to accept the inherent limitations of sociology itself. Though the sociologist may admit that there is incomprehensibility and mystery about the individual as a living being, he is apt to imply that social habits and institutions are the whole "cause" or explanation of the individual. But no amount of explaining the limitations and conditions surrounding life can really deal with the reality of life itself, or gainsay such actual experiences as those of loving, or enjoying, of the warmness in sympathy or the pang in suffering. Those are not to be translated into lesser terms, but are elemental in a Wordsworthian sense. Sociological and psychological knowledge remain external, descriptive and explanatory in character.

The fact is that though the sociologist may make us more keenly aware of some of the ways in which social groups behave, he cannot, as a sociologist, give us a real purpose in living. For one thing, such a purpose must always have

[2] Page 169.

within it a lively knowledge of what it feels like to wonder, to laugh, to will—in a word, what it feels like to be a person. And so, with all our sociological knowledge and all the consciousness it has brought us of the influence of society upon our growth, we shall still be left with an unsatisfactory idea of the real scope of education because we shall not have seen that education is concerned with men as living, feeling and potentially individual people and not merely members of a society. We may see the need for a wide and interesting education; we shall hardly be shown the need for an education in depth.

In working out a contemporary philosophy of education, we must certainly take very seriously much that the anthropologists, psychologists and sociologists tell us about the laws of individual and social development, the limitations of possibility for man in many directions. On the other hand, we must take with equal seriousness the no less veritable evidences brought in by the "obstinate questionings" of our own hearts; the common experience of men and women that life is not simply a duration in time but has deeps and shallows; our sudden insights that values have an eternal element within them and that there is a real meaning in things. There are several *sorts* of facts to be faced and so often today the scientists face some kinds and artists and religious men other kinds. A knowledge and examination of the outside of facts or of ideas is no substitute at all for a knowledge of them from the inside. And it is with the outside of facts and ideas that scientists must always deal, the psychologists and sociologists no less than the physicists.

"The physicists," says Karl Jaspers, "tell us the history of the universe. With the primal explosion began that process which to astronomers of our time manifests itself in the recession of the astral nebulae as the still continuously expanding universe. Anyone who hears of this, together with the factual evidence, stands amazed before this cosmos now so summarily explained, and thinks, perhaps, that now we know how it all began. Wherever measurements and mathematics predominate modern man is inclined to submit. . . . But the world is not only the astronomical cosmos as discerned by measurements, convincing as far as they are verifiable, in terms of mathematical abstractions, and hence necessarily thought of as lifeless. That there is life and that we are human beings and that there arises a consciousness for which all this becomes comprehensible to an illimitable degree, all this we can no more infer today from our purely mathematical knowledge of the world than we could formerly from the mechanism of the play of atoms. From the perceptible cosmos we cannot infer the origin of the thought which perceives it." [3]

Man himself does not really *create* life, though men undoubtedly beget children and women are undoubtedly the vehicles of their birth. There is an inexplicable mystery in the whole process, the production of a result which is more than the sum of the causes and never entirely prophesiable from them. Creation, as it were, is still going on by the operation of forces of which human beings are some of the media.

It is extremely difficult for us, embedded in our own period of time, to feel, or even to see, that a detached, scientific attitude is only one of the attitudes which we need

[a] *The Listener*, 26 June 1952.

if we are to face life honestly or intelligently. The very difficulty our minds have in realizing this is a measure of the power of a climate of opinion over us. The scientist, as such, can have no values other than the pursuit of definable truth. Beauty and self-sacrifice and religion are inevitably for him, as a scientist, simply more material for analysis. Many men will argue with passion that beauty is not *real* in the sense that scientific truth is real—or, alternatively, that beauty can be composed and made once we know the rules. Beauty itself is only a matter of arranging words or notes of music or colours or shapes. Schönberg indeed has made up music on these principles and is a distinguished composer, typically modern. As for religion, it is a very common view that it should be seen as a defence mechanism or a consequence of the retention into grown-up years of a childhood fantasy and unconscious feeling of need for a father. But of all men the thorough-going determinist must be the most miserable, when he sees himself as he demonstrably appears to be: confined within the universe with no power save that of obedience to its definable laws, physical, sociological, economic.

The escape from the cage can only come by our acceptance and acknowledgment of a conviction that there are other kinds of knowledge than the kind which scientific observation and the most careful analysis of data will yield. What do we mean by "knowledge"? Normally the term is used in so narrow a sense that we have no word left to cover a good deal of what we ought to mean by the term. By knowledge we usually mean: (i) Factual knowledge about things or events. Two plus two makes four; Queen Elizabeth the First died in 1603; Boston is north of New

York. (ii) Knowledge about how to do things. This is, of course, knowledge of a different sort or species—but it is demonstrable, finite. We know, for example, how to fasten a safety pin; how to get from the bedroom to the dining-room in our house. (iii) Knowledge of people. Here the word is used in a more subtle way. We know John or Joan not merely because we can identify them, but because experience has taught us that they will behave in particular ways—that, for instance, you could lend one of them a five-dollar bill with perfect safety, but not the other.

But what of other sorts of knowledge? To listen to the symphonies of Sibelius so that they become really a part of us is surely to add to our knowledge—not only in the superficial sense that by so doing we learn to recognize passage after passage, and can adumbrate the pattern of the whole whenever we hear a part of the music again, but in the more profound sense that, because the music has meant so much to us, we have been modified by it in our very nature and outlook. Our listening has brought us not a transitory experience, to be easily rubbed out, but "knowledge" which has changed us. Religious knowledge in the full, experiential sense is obviously very different from knowing about the events of religious history or knowing a creed by heart. Real affection for John or for Joan can give us a "knowledge" of them which is not ever to be captured fully by words, but is true knowledge nevertheless, though of a kind which may cease to be ours if we stop loving them.

No amount of knowledge about beauty will add up to the knowledge of beauty given by a single experience of a mountain landscape or a Mozart sonata. No amount of knowledge *about* religion, or religions primitive or Christian, is any substitute for knowledge *of* religion—i.e. religious experience. But the difficulty is not to be overcome by a logical argument with the man to whom objective knowledge is the only real knowledge. Perhaps it can only be overcome by feeding and nourishing his experiencing power and by helping him to realize slowly that he does in fact tacitly recognize other values than objective truth in loving his sweetheart or wife and children, in acknowledging the value of unselfishness and of high courage, in enjoying a sunset. He may still, indeed, in spite of such evidences continue to declare that these experiences anyway are unimportant and in the ultimate sense unreal.

If we look at human groups and human beings simply from the outside, we shall inevitably fail—and fail hopelessly—to understand them. It is only too easy by a process of external classification and analysis to squeeze experiences dry of all their juice and so to depersonalize the world. A favourite process in these days is to reduce experiences so that they become merely abstract classifications. Love may be seen only as sexuality; thought as only the result of chemical processes; decisions as only the outcome of social forces. And thus things always seem to be in the saddle and always to be riding mankind. But by its very nature sociology deals chiefly with one dimension of experience, with the threads of reality rather than the whole cloth, with trends and tendencies and laws of behaviour rather than with growing points in the individual —acts of will, battles in the conscience, fear and passion and devotion with all their cost. Science states true propositions about the world, but much truth can never be expressed in the form of propositions at all; it is multidimensional, life warm and in the round. There is a sense in which the flat is the unprofitable too. To assume that observations which can be set down in clear words or language are more real and important than experiences which cannot is obviously foolish. A railway time-table is not more important than a painting by Corot, but differently so. The quest of science is the eternal human quest for certainty in its modern guise—and if we really found what we appear to be seeking, life would have no inwardness, no content, and no point.

To the actual individual learning to be a good member of society life must be an experiential, existential business. At first, as William James said long ago in a famous phrase, it comes upon the baby as a big, blooming, buzzing confusion: that is, not simply a big confusion, but a confusion that is an experience too. Every life is made up of a succession of actual situations in which we are involved as persons at deeper or shallower levels. We begin life not simply by being members of a social group—to believe that and that only is to look at things abstractly and in one dimension alone—but by knowing and loving a particular father with a bushy moustache and one special, understanding mother, and maybe our brother Tom and our sister Mary too. It is through intensely personal experiences such as these that we learn to understand the human world outside us: we certainly could not even faintly understand remorse or jealousy or laughter in others unless we had felt something like them welling up within ourselves. We grow up within a family, within a social class, within a particular nation at a particular period of time, only gradually, if ever, becoming consciously aware of more than bits of our environment. And at the same time we may well be growing up recognizably English or American, twentieth century, middle class.

But nothing that is observed in detachment—scientifically—can deny the real and actual feelings we have as we enjoy and experience life. We may be easily recognizable as members of a society, but all the time we are breathing, sensitive men or women too. Nor can a "society" experience love or sorrow instead of us or instead of anybody at all. It is the individual who is real; a collection of individuals is an abstraction, a description. No doubt the ways in which any individual comes to feel, to express himself, to will, and to act are largely governed by the ways in which other people in his society, and in particular special groups of people within it, have taught him how to feel, to express himself, to determine and to do. But the feelings and the actions are nevertheless his own and genuinely spontaneous—springing from within him—however much their pattern may be seen, if we look at it externally, simply to reproduce that of surrounding society.

2

We have not educated men more than a little when we have made them more literate, more vocal and more technically skilled. The school has to nourish and educate feeling and intelligence and will, as well as to impart knowledge and techniques and to train minds, each according to its capacity, to analyze and dissect. Education is concerned with producing attitudes, and this means not teaching in so many words the desirability of attitudes, but making a really personal contact and "entry." Its business is to help men actually to feel, to think and to act, not merely to teach them *what* to feel, *what* to think and *when* to act. Its concern in other words is with people not only as functionaries in a society but as individuals and persons. For however much alike the deeds of men in the same social group may seem to be, when observed from without, to the degree that men are real they are individual and personal. There is no society so perfect as to take away from any man within it the need for being and for doing good. No man can ever act with sincerity without acting as an individual; and sincerity is not merely genuineness, it is originality too, though this is not, of course, to deny that only a few exceptional people in any age—a Columbus, a Galileo, a Karl Marx, a Freud—will by their originality contribute something new and different to society from that given to it by the originality of other people.

Some societies or nations are far more rigidly conventional than others. But every group permits some freedom of initiative and imagination and is willing in the long run to incorporate new contributions from the individual, provided that they are contributions of an acceptable sort. What is worthy of the name individuality is to be attained only by livingly entering into the humanity and normality of one's society, embodying that and going beyond it. Socrates was profoundly and typically an Athenian, though the Athenians put him to death, but he was intensely an individual and a pioneer too; and eventually his notions and discoveries were incorporated within the main stream of Greek thought and the thought of the West. If, however, a man aims at individuality as an end in itself, he will tend

to develop not true individuality but eccentricity and odd-
ness. If a school aims at individuality in its pupils as an end
in itself it may turn out some very peculiar children. That
indeed is where the experimental school, built on a philosophy of *laissez-faire*, sometimes goes wrong. For by educating for individuality as in itself the goal, it mistakes means
for end. The way to become really a member of a society is
by living and experiencing within it, as the recipe for becoming a scout is first to be of the right age, and then to
throw oneself into scouting, dressing as a scout, going to
meetings of the troop, loving to go on hikes and to camps
with one's fellow scouts, graduating through the hierarchy
of badges.

There is in fact no recipe for becoming really an individual save by loving, suffering, experiencing, thinking
and responsibly planning ahead, as other men do within
the great school of love and suffering and experience
which one's society runs. And perhaps it is true that the
less secure a society, the more important is the individual's
embodiment within himself of something of its historic
faith and purpose; and that is not to be gained in any sec-
ondhand, copybook way.

To sum up. Along the current of sociological thought
very much has come to us that needed bringing. We are
compelled now to take far more account of the unconscious presuppositions which form so much of education
and affect us in so many ways. We are forced against the
delusions of self-interest to reckon with the power of group
loyalty, group bias, group taboo to command the individual
to feel and think and act. These must be reckoned with at
least as much as the effects of drink and drugs upon the

capacity to learn, or the need for food and rest and exercise in matters of health.

The limitations of the sociological approach to the study of education are the limitations of any objective and scientific approach. Of necessity, and rightly, sociology leaves out of its account the sharp experience and reality of living. It can have no criteria at last for evaluating the relative worth of different societies, for its concern is with studying them and not estimating their value. It leaves the individual man or woman out of its reckoning and is not concerned with the effort of the individual to perceive or to do right rather than wrong.

Sociological study does nothing to make moral effort any less necessary for man or beauty any less real. No one can live simply as a sociologist, and no man or woman really alive is in the position of being an automaton or simply a slave of social laws. He has choices to make that are really choices; what he becomes tomorrow will in part surely depend on what he decides today. A society can on the whole be civilized or uncivilized, morally awake or morally comatose, materially energetic or just lazy. But almost certainly some sections of it will be more civilized than others, more kindhearted, more moral, more energetic. And while the job of the statesman is to secure that as far as possible those are the sections given power, the job of the educator is to secure that as far as possible those are the sections given most responsibility for educating the young.

4

INHERITING TRADITIONS

1

In the second half of this book we must apply some of these reflections rather more closely to the actual business of educating. But before we can do that we must face fairly and squarely the important question—raised implicitly in the last chapter—of the place of indoctrination in education.

In a well-known passage in his *Table Talk*, Coleridge recounts that his friend Thelwall thought it very unfair to influence a child's mind by inculcating any opinions before it should have come to years of discretion, and be able to choose for itself. "I showed him my garden, and told him it was my botanical garden. 'How so?' said he, 'it is covered with weeds'—'Oh,' I replied, '*that* is only because it has not yet come to its age of discretion and choice. The weeds, you see, have taken the liberty to grow, and I thought it unfair in me to prejudice the soil towards roses and straw-berries!' " [1]

The process of helping people to incorporate the pattern and traditions of their society is, of course, a process of biasing. And it is one from which there is no escape. It is not carried on through words only; nor should it be regarded only as the imparting of formally defined doctrines. The process of indoctrination may make use of words, but it is not only the words that will matter or the accuracy of the listening: the tone of the utterance and the frame of mind of the listener are important elements in what is going to be understood by the words that are said. A comedian is careful to prepare an audience for the joke he is going to make, or they may hardly perceive it as a joke. A mother instinctively teaches her baby to believe in her own devotion and love, in her trustworthiness and friendliness. What she actually says is but a very small part of the teaching she gives. The way she looks at her child, smiles at it, touches it so that each touch is a caress or a reproof, all are parts of her communication with it and to it. She understands the meaning of its sudden momentary gazes and the wobbly turning of its head; and the baby feels that she understands, as nobody else does.

Even in the school we cannot teach information and knowledge and skills and techniques by themselves. We cannot in fact possibly teach in a neat and tidy isolation just what we are seeking to teach—and no more. When we were at school we all learnt much from our masters or mistresses which they had no idea at all they were teaching us. Men may be remorselessly efficient schoolmasters, who con-

[1] *Table Talk:* 27 July 1830.

centrate ruthlessly on the matter in hand, but inevitably their high or low evaluation of the importance of the examination ahead, their choice to neglect beauty for the sake of analysis, their scholarliness, their urgent or lack of urgent sense of purpose, will get over too—meaning and mattering to children in different proportions and degrees according to the children's own background and temperaments and the stage of development they have reached.

It is impossible to teach without conveying all sorts of beliefs and evaluations simply by implication. No society ever taught its younger generation the truth about its own history. Mixed up in any possible teaching of Byron or Brahms or the Bible are value judgments. Try to read Wordsworth, or play Mozart, antiseptically, so that no germs of our own enjoyment shall infect our pupils; can the essentials be taught thus or are they simply left out? Try to conduct morning prayers with a cold detachment: will they be prayers at all?

Quite fundamentally important in all education given in home or school are the ideas and ideals we teach at the pre-conceptual level, almost without knowing that we are teaching them. It is indeed in this way that we teach the characteristic ethos of our civilization. By the term indoctrination we usually mean the conscious and systematic teaching of opinions (particularly political opinions) or creeds (particularly religious creeds) to other people. Doctrines have been thought of as if they were almost, if not quite, completely expressible in words. But this is too simple and ingenuous an interpretation of the process and involves some very questionable assumptions.

One assumption is that the doctrines or beliefs which

matter most could be fully formulated and brought into consciousness if we wished. Another is that education, as carried on in schools and higher institutions of learning, need, if we tried hard enough, have little concern with indoctrination at all. Indeed in many countries it is held that while it is legitimate for a church or a political party to indoctrinate, the school and the university must and should be "neutral," the implication being that this is not only desirable but possible. One of the main jobs of the school and college, it is claimed, is to teach skills (reading, writing, arithmetic and the many more advanced skills built upon them); another is to teach knowledge in the form of facts—geographical, historical, scientific, linguistic; and a third to teach the importance of reasoning and of reason. But with the fostering of beliefs and attitudes it need have little to do.

And yet, as we have seen, the findings of anthropology, sociology and in large measure psychology have during the past forty years increasingly pointed to the impossibility of our continuing to hold this position. A society preserves its unity and its very existence by so orientating its members that they take a good many of the same things for granted and share together a good many of the same tenets. The culture within which men live limits their very imaginations, and we must honestly face the fact.

The distinction between doctrines that are consciously formulated and consciously imparted and doctrines that are held suspended in the atmosphere and take the form of "climates of value and opinion" is a less important distinction than is often imagined. Everyone has to be deeply and significantly indoctrinated from very early in life if he is going really to be a member of any community or nation. The attitudes we learn from parents and society are such as to make certain kinds of learning forever afterwards possible, or difficult, or not possible at all. Schools, and even universities, exist largely to perpetuate those elements in our civilization which the sections of society "behind" them regard as important. If nobody is "behind" a school, if nobody really believes in the education it is giving, it cannot be a very potent place. That, maybe, is what is wrong with quite a number of schools today.

T. E. Hulme in his seminal book *Speculations* argues that the assumptions which we make in arriving at particular judgments pass unnoticed because they lie at a deep level in the unconscious mind. They colour not merely our judgments on a particular issue, but our whole way of looking at things. We do not see them but we see other things through them. They will determine the very questions we allow ourselves to ask, as well as the answers we find satisfactory to those questions. All the time we are teaching a child's conscious mind we are—often without meaning to do so—forming and influencing his motives and attitudes, building within him values and standards.

In the process of absorption of a culture the long years of infancy and childhood are extremely important. By the age of fourteen the child will inevitably have been inoculated by influences which will cause him to believe good or less good things of his country; to catch a high moral standard or a low one from those around him; to incline towards or away from the idea that the individual human personality has rights which can outweigh those of the state; to behave (if he is a boy) more or less as a boy is expected to behave in his society, or (if she is a girl) more or less as a girl is expected to behave. The school, of course, is only one of the media for thus indoctrinating the child: the street, the motion picture, advertisements, newspapers, friends, are others. Even the choice by parents of the suburb in which they shall go to live is an educational choice.

Much of the underlying purpose of education is to help the growing citizen to become more fully the possessor of the traditions which vitalize his society. Through his education he comes to inherit beliefs in which to grow to maturity, beliefs which are nourishing, indeed essential, to growth, including ones about his own nature and its capabilities.

But if so much of the education we absorb—whether in institutions of learning or outside them—carries indoctrination in it and with it, how shall we escape? Can we never put off the blinkers which growing up in any particular society must impose? Is there no such thing as "pure" education? These questions are only to be asked after we have faced the truth that we need to believe as much as we need to learn facts. The ultimate purpose of education cannot be to help us to become detached spectators, whether of ourselves or of the world. If the aim of a "pure" education were to help us to be reasonable in the sense of permanently uninvolved and permanently neutral, it would be an absurd and unreal aim.

And yet undoubtedly one of the capacities it is highly desirable to foster, at least from adolescence onwards, is a capacity for detached judgment. It is upon a deliberate effort to be neutral and look at things temporarily from the outside that our science and our justice have been built.

What we must beware of is the unwarranted assumption that it is possible to take an attitude of detachment all the time, or that it would yield us the "truth" if it were. No one can fall in love detachedly. It is meaningless to talk about enjoying a sunset or a symphony of Beethoven's without involvement, or of worshipping God "neutrally." It is extremely important to learn to be as unprejudiced as is humanly possible in a laboratory, a mathematical lecture room or a court of law; but the detached and analytic approach to experience and to life is nevertheless only sometimes relevant—and even then involves belief: an unshakable belief in the value of truth and justice. We may be neutral at times in the laboratory, but to be permanently neutral and without beliefs about things that matter—war or religion or cruelty to animals or the virtue of our daughter—is to be less, not more, than human. It is a question whether any teacher in a school *can* teach some of the most important things—about the arts, philosophy, politics—in a detached, uninvolved way, just "historically and objectively."

It is certainly important to learn how to be neutral on occasion at will; to learn how to weigh evidence in detachment; to learn as far as is humanly possible to be unprejudiced. But it is wrong to think that learning these things is education and the chief duty of man, whereas learning beliefs and how to behave inwardly according to good traditions within one's society is not profoundly the business of education too. By analysis and in detachment one can learn much about life, but only by living can one learn how to live. He is not the best friend to civilization who sacrifices his humanity and finds himself at last committed to believing in nothing but verifiable facts, having in the course of years become an expert instead of a human being. The ordinary man distrusts the expert, the specialist, because he suspects their neutrality to be an escape from real living. The real justification for being at times detached and neutral about any issue is that deep within us we have faith in truth, a passion to find out the real truth and not be misled by an opinion or convention that we can allow for. Yet a life of permanent neutrality or uncommitment is unlivable. It is only in certain circumstances that we can judge entirely on the evidence before us and nothing but that evidence. Even justice is done largely by reference to tradition.

Neutrality—life in an ivory tower even with all modern conveniences, including positivist shower-baths—is to be achieved only on the way to involvement. To think of it as the goal, rather than simply, in the words of Professor Arnaud Reid, as the moment between breathing out and breathing in, is in fact in the long run to find merely an up-to-date, Western substitute for Nirvana. Caring for something and caring a great deal, and having a desire that others should care too—these are essential to a life well lived. The more important we really feel life to be, the more involved in it we are compelled to become. The completely neutral, "unbiased" man eventually has to choose by the toss of a coin. It is by a natural process of indoctrination, of passing on the vision and the dream, that many of the gains of civilization are preserved; maybe it is only upon the rocks of doctrine that we can build even our neutralities.

2

And yet, of course, some very large questions remain. Are we to be for the most part slaves of whatever doctrines we inherit or pick up from our society? Have we no freedom with which to choose good beliefs rather than less good? Can we choose with some freedom right ways of being involved? Though the education of the young may include a good deal of conditioning is it really moral deliberately and consciously to pass on "doctrines" to them? Often, of course, we shall not be aware that we are doing it, nor by any exercise of introspection within our power can we make ourselves aware. But inevitably the more civilized we become the more conscious we shall be of the subtlety with which we do in fact inculcate this value-judgment or that, this belief or that non-belief. And in consequence the more we shall be unable to avoid facing the question: is it right to "bias" the young when we know that we are doing it?

I believe not only that we are thoroughly justified in biasing and influencing our children to have standards, to be courageous and to believe in truth and freedom, but also that it is our absolute obligation to do so. We must not be afraid of educating for commitment. What matters is that the philosophy of life we set growing in our children should be one which reckons with human greatness, with the growing points within each individual, and with the capacity of men to reach to moments of real decision. The choice is not between neutrality and a faith: it is, first, choice between a greater or a lesser consciousness of the faith and the values to which we do in fact hold and which do in fact impel us, and it is, secondly, the choice between a faith which has more understanding of the sweep of human experience and a faith which takes less of human experience into account.

We have to inherit—and come to accept willingly and personally—much of the general cultural pattern of our society. We have also to fit ourselves into and accept much of the particular cultural pattern made by the various parts of that society to which we belong and the various classes within it of which we are members. But still we are often presented with choices which we have to make as individuals and which no one can make for us—choices which have to be made if for no other reason (though there may be other reasons) than that the parts or classes of the society to which we belong overlap. Within every society there are more civilized and less civilized strands, more civilized and less civilized traditions of thought and behaviour. We each have some freedom to choose which of those strands we shall follow within ourselves. We all have a certain choice of adherence between traditions equally alive within our society. It is possible to act, as a business man frequently acts, with self-interest or the advancement of the interest of his firm looming large among his motives. Inventions can be suppressed which might benefit mankind, because they would render obsolete the products of one's own firm. Or it is possible to act more honestly, morally and disinterestedly than that—as scientists, educated and helped by the ethos of their profession, normally do, at any rate in their scientific work. The decisions which individual men make at key points in their lives about which of the traditions of their society they shall follow within themselves and, therefore, in due course influence others to follow, are highly significant decisions.

How then shall we arrive at a good and responsible choice of a line of action or thought? It is only within limits, as I have been suggesting, that we can consciously choose. Is it not true to experience that for the most part in human life we do not change our tastes; rather we find them changed? We do not change our beliefs with forethought and deliberation; rather we find that they do not satisfy us in quite their old form. But times do come when we have to make a decision and make it quite consciously. We have to choose which of two social traditions, at work with almost equal power within us, we shall follow, and this may involve bringing up for conscious consideration some of the habits, ideas and ideals which might otherwise have remained unconscious in our minds. It may be only a small matter: shall we, for instance, pronounce this or that word with a local accent or a national one? Shall we say "right poorly" or "very ill"? Or it may be something rather more important: shall we play tennis or football on Sundays? Shall we send our child to the local public school or to a private school at a greater distance from home? A choice to settle the issue has to be made. There are questions of principle which we have to decide at many times in life: and the decision essentially is always whether we shall act according to this tradition or tendency within us or according to that—to economize or to spend; to be merciful or refrain from mercy; to sin or not to sin.

The man who is truly responsible is one who has come as personally, as actively and as consciously as he can to share the values which make his civilization civilized. The person we habitually think of as "educated" is very much this representative, comprehensive man. The "educated" man or woman is one who incorporates the best that is thought and known in his world. But more than that, he is a man capable of acting from what he incarnates, that is of taking responsibility, when called upon, as an alone individual.

> "Only by acceptance of the past
> Will you alter its meaning,"

says a character in *The Family Reunion*. Such an acceptance is an individual business. Yet we must have been put by our education into a position from which we can perceive what has to be accepted.

In the long run education is concerned with bringing people to points where they can with a clear sight accept as theirs most of the values to which their own ancestors have held. This is not a matter only of learning facts but of coming to experience; and if facts are one-dimensional, experiences can be many-dimensional. It is they which fertilize the spirit. For everyone coming into a real experience and absorbing it, it must be true that

> "He was the first that ever burst
> Into that silent sea."

Right education must include the development of the capacity for this conscious act of acceptance. The most educated person, as distinct from the best trained or the most informed, is the one who has most fully, freshly and livingly absorbed the "doctrines"—not simply this item from a creed or that item, but a whole still growing outlook, a whole and still living philosophy. To use a Platonic metaphor, he has been gradually turned to the light by his education and is now able, really as a person, to accept his world.

In most judgments which matter, the way to right and responsible choosing is not the way of a neutral, detached and external judgment, but the way of a more central, comprehending and profound involvement. To be godlike is to be most warmly involved, not to be most coldly detached. It is a mistake to identify subjectivity with selfishness and objectivity with unselfishness. Such entry and understanding is the very opposite of selfishness. Some truths have to happen to us if we are to see that they are truths, and these come to the receptive mind rather than to the analytical one. Many of the experiences most worth having are not to be had at all unless we are prepared to be proved wrong by what we experience. We have to go deeper than the desire to be proved right. This is not detachment; another name for it is humility. But such involvement will not be possible without an intimate learning of the disciplines and the inspirations known to good men in one's society.

Yet though neutrality may be a moment in the process of understanding, the achievement of understanding is the goal. We begin by becoming indoctrinated; to the extent to which we fully grow up we become responsible for the doctrines—and for modifying and restating them. The only escape from this situation is by ceasing to be human.

3

But have I been saying that all indoctrination is good? By no means. Indoctrination of the sort about which I have en writing does not conflict with the freedom or the humanity of people in the only sense in which freedom and humanity are real. Indoctrination of this kind is part of the very process of growing to be mature in any conceivable human culture or society. It is a continuation of the process of growing into a fully human being which took place physically in the nine months before we were born. But now it is the culture of our society which is the womb, and the spirit not the body which is gestated. The product of this sort of education and indoctrination is an individual in his degree personally responsible for the culture which he has inherited and responsible too for adding to its content and changing its direction as called for by the times in which he lives. To be content to think of social change purely in terms of trends and not in terms of personal responsibility is in the long run dishonest.

One of the first principles of teaching must be to intend and will that as many children as possible shall be able by adolescence to reach to moments when they can choose for themselves between this tradition or that growing within them—to "fall for" a Mozart sonata with its human love and understanding or to "fall for" a Strauss waltz with its reluctance and romance, to yield to the tide of popular judgment and opinion or to defy it, to run with the rabble or to make a stand for order. There is a great difference between unquestioning acceptance of other people's opinions and a growth into accepting for oneself an opinion nascent within. A child's freedom to choose between traditions within him may be more limited than we used to imagine, but the essential freedom is freedom to fight a battle within the self and to win or lose it, alone.

If our long-term aim is simply to compel children to accept from the outside a faith ready-made and to take over by rote, at second-hand, a set of values which they do not gradually come to feel as their own, we are not in fact educating them to be fully human. We must so educate and encourage them that they bring up into consciousness the faith they hold, accepting it and modifying it in the light of reason. For an act of personal acceptance is necessary, repeatedly renewed as circumstances change and life goes on. This act will be the more intimately personal the more intelligent and awake a man is; both his heart and his head have their part in it.

All this does not mean, of course, that simply because we want to give the child scope for choosing we should give him endless battles to fight, or battles that are too difficult for him to win. If we honestly believe that whisky is bad for him, that atheism does not face life truthfully, that honesty is important, it will be irresponsible to encourage the child to believe otherwise. Indeed we can hardly really be said to love him, whether we be parents or teachers, if we deliberately try to encourage in him a faith we do not in large measure share.

But in actual fact it is in any case exceedingly difficult, if not impossible, to do this. For, as was said earlier, the beliefs we really succeed in imparting are not the ones we may teach with our lips, if our lives and insinuations subtly contradict them. Parent and child, learner and teacher, must be in close relationship if the young are going to learn save in a superficial, one-dimensional sense. There must be a "certain weight of common assumption" between them.

The second principle on which a teacher should proceed

is that children should be educated so that they will become responsible as individual persons for continuing civilization themselves in due course, each in his degree becoming an incarnation of it and of the lines of development within it. This involves sharing experiences and finding a meaning within those experiences akin to the meaning which the great have found.

It is the great men of a civilization—its poets, creative administrators, saints, statesmen, scientists—who are the real makers and preservers of standards. They are not only embodiments of tradition: it is they who extend the line of belief. They discover more of the meaning of civilization and freedom because they are so much "inside" life, not because they are its spectators, detachedly, from the outside. And the test of greatness is whether men continue to find those with a reputation for being great the source of richness in themselves. The ultimate criterion of greatness or goodness or beauty can only be deeds and books and works of art which men still repeatedly feel to be beautiful, good or great. But what they feel to be beautiful and right proves in actual fact to have a good deal in common with what men within that society—and perhaps many other societies too—have down the ages felt to be so.

There is a great difference, however, between such indispensable, far-reaching indoctrination and the use of propaganda for self-interested purposes. To try by propaganda or the use of fear or the arts of the advertiser to modify beliefs or actions which spring from deep within a humane culture can be a betrayal of humanity itself. The test of the goodness of a doctrine is its quality and depth. The test, in other words, is how much richness of human experience, and truth to the nature of things, and intelligence, it incorporates and continues to embody. Admittedly, it is not always easy to apply the test. And our ability to apply it must depend upon our own recognition of the profound when we encounter it. I am told that in judging character through handwriting the first thing to do is to look for signs of the general high or mediocre or low quality in the writer—indicated, it is said, through spacing, proportion, originality or lack of originality in making letter-forms. According to the general class, particular features will mean this or that or something quite different. There is a similar distinction between what I have called indoctrination and what I have called propaganda. Everything depends on the level of the mind from which they spring. There is an element of the brutal about mere propaganda. Sometimes, without doubt, it is necessary to use it, on the principle "Might till right is ready." A child must on occasion forcibly be prevented from touching the bright bars of the electric fire with an enquiring hand. Propagandist injunctions even to grown-ups may often be justified: "Danger, you have been warned!" "Go slow, see our town; go fast, see our jail" or "Eat more fruit." But the effect of much propaganda of this kind is to anaesthetize the judgment and to keep people at best adolescent. The power to indulge in propaganda is always dangerous when in the possession of the criminal, the uncivilized, the seekers of power, the inhumane—and it is they perhaps who are most tempted to use it.

The essential difference between indoctrination and propaganda lies in the different evaluations of human nature they make: the one is without fundamental respect, the other reckons with the essential humanity in man. There are vast possibilities of social control in the utilization of modern techniques of propaganda, perfected by psychological knowledge and by recently invented devices for the large-scale influencing of opinion—motion pictures, radio, television, the use of emotional atmosphere and symbols, the censoring and arranging of news, the leading of mass movements. The aim of the propagandist is to compel someone else to behave as he wishes: the propagandist has no reverence for the "otherness" of the one he is trying to influence and no desire to see him become really responsible or mature. There is a cynicism about propaganda: it makes use of other people, either blatantly or subtly, for the propagandist's own purposes. And the propagandist is not likely to be one who himself has really entered far into the civilization to which he belongs. He is salesman rather than priest. Propaganda assumes that people have no great depths from which to give themselves, and so they can be managed, directed, manipulated. It does not really *believe* in people at all. It uses them. It treats them as material, instead of—however incompletely mature they may be—as boys and girls, men and women. Its aim is to make people more like animals or machines than they were before.

The growth of men and women to maturity is bound to be a slow process and there are severe limits to what one can do to make it go on faster. Much education is a process of inheriting and of learning about one's inheritance; of becoming indoctrinated and of raising some part of the "doctrines" into consciousness. To be human is to have had relatives and ancestors: it is a great thing even to belong to the same race of beings as Rembrandt or Einstein, as Abraham Lincoln or Alfred North Whitehead. But as growth proceeds very slowly, so does the process of realizing one's responsibilities. They stretch away from one in many directions, and they are something like limbs: for they are to our spiritual body as limbs are to our physical one. To become responsible and to act responsibly are unconditional demands. No one really can take responsibility upon himself without pouring himself, or some of himself, into an action: it cannot as a real responsibility be externally stuck on. Responsibilities have to be accepted before they are seen as responsibilities. Responsibility, therefore, is genuineness, and—because no one can act without committing himself—in a very real sense of the word, originality. And from responsibility, accepted at a deep enough level, comes leadership.

Propaganda, on the other hand, has little to do with education. It treats human beings as if they were robots actuated by self-interest. The business of education is to make us gradually into persons, and to the degree of our intelligence conscious of our duties. We have first to absorb what Professor Hodges of Reading University has called "a sense of context and public purpose in the marrow of our bones"; and then, roughly in proportion to the range of our intelligence, become conscious of why we do things and of the directions in which change must be brought about to modify tradition. To us as individuals it may fall to change the direction of the world's development but slightly; but we are not likely to do it at all unless we do it from the inside.

Between commitment and true freedom there is no contradition and the world today is in great need of both. What is dehumanizing is a commitment to some creed or faith, poor in quality and in understanding of the greatness of God and of the potential greatness of human nature itself. Neutrality in the sense of a detachment from attitude and belief is impossible: but the individual has power to choose between higher and lower sincerities in himself—and the choice matters. It is in the individual that the battle for human development is taking place. There is nowhere else in which it could conceivably be fought.

Education thus must be not only a training in conformity, but a preparation for acting alone—even if the acts looked at afterwards, from the outside, appear to be conformist. There is all the difference between educating people so that they are compelled to obey, and educating them so that their own spirits, the deeply individual "I" in each, are involved in the obedience—or in that disobedience which is an extension of obedience, not a contradiction of it.

4

In this chapter we began by talking about indoctrination, and have found ourselves long before the end talking about freedom. Essential freedom, we have said, is freedom to fight a battle within the self and to win or lose it, alone. Granted that most of our life is determined for us rather than by us, that we act out of custom and habit rather than from any really individual and central part of ourselves, do there not come to us, if but rarely, times when we know that much is at stake, when a decisive

choice has to be consciously made and when not to be involved is to betray our own humanity? A choice made at
such a time is creative of selfhood, not only an expression
of it. We may not be able to justify in words what we do
at a moment of decision. "At such an hour we live the
eternal life in the midst of time; past, present and future
are not dimensions in which we live; we are their master
and fuse them into the unity of a single creative action." [2]

Most of life is an escape from freedom and we had better acknowledge, conscious of our human limitation, that
this must be so. We occupy ourselves in doing things, we
talk and amuse ourselves, we are led on intriguingly by
our curiosities, we learn to become adepts at concealing
our impulses and feelings, not merely from other people
but from ourselves. And all this is inevitable. We are not
strong enough to be or to do otherwise. Indeed the very
possibility of winning moments of selfhood, of loneliness
or of understanding must depend upon the safety given us
by society; and if we are not loyal to society and do not
remain more or less normal members of it there could be
no protection for the individual. It is not surprising that
the sociologist, viewing and studying boys and girls or men
and women from the outside, will in nine cases out of ten
—if he is observant enough and clever enough—be right in
his forecasts of the actions and behaviour of Mr. A. and
Mrs. B., of Miss C. or Master D., whose society and whose
upbringing he has been studying with so much method and
so much care. Most people for most of the time do prophesiable things. Civilization still needs the herd-instinct. In
unity still is strength.

[2] E. L. Allen, *Existentialism from Within*, p. 126.

But this must not blind us to the fact that there is no wisdom and no freedom in conventionality or gregariousness. To learn how to talk so that we may escape from quietness; to exercise curiosity so that we may escape from mystery; to use the arts of concealment and manœuvre, in flight from being real, is to say "No" to life and not "Yes." So often men rush into action because they cannot bear the burden of experiencing; or the burden of being responsible. But it is themselves they are running away from.

For the most part schooling must needs be concentrated upon teaching people how to do things—to read, write and add; to plane and cook and sew; to pass examinations and win successes in the world of achievement and of action, successes which are necessary on the one hand to self-respect in society and on the other to the earning of daily bread. But these are not the only ends of education. Even a perfect inheriting of the best traditions of our society and a perfect learning to fit in with social custom is not enough. The goal is not a perfection of adaptation to the accepted any more than it is an infinity of knowledge; rather it is a preparation of the self for being able, at occasional moments, to be free.

How shall this be done? First, parent and teacher, however severe their discipline or definite their instruction, must themselves acknowledge the child's humanity and otherness from them, his potentiality to attain to moments of freedom, his right so to come into touch with his own centre that he shall be able to act upon occasion as an individual. Secondly, his capacity for inward experiencing must be preserved throughout his whole training, not prevented or ridiculed or starved. Thirdly, he must be encouraged to keep the ability, which early shines in him, to convey experience to others as experience. Fourthly, there must be an education of his sense of belonging, and there must be a training, and a sharpening, of the will. These suggestions will be annotated in the chapters which follow.

5

DISCIPLINE AND INDIVIDUALITY

1

It is clear that in practice the first means of ensuring what education a child receives is to exercise a control over the groups and sub-groups to which he is allowed to belong. In a good home the friends with whom a child is encouraged to mix, the comics he is permitted to take, the motion pictures he is allowed to see, are to some extent at least under parental control. And so are the parts of his parents' own minds and hearts into which he is given an entry. If we want children to develop imagination and humanity, they must be brought up among people who are themselves imaginative and humane, or given some chance of coming into touch with them. Children, and indeed grown-ups, can only to a very small extent have knowledge of possible attitudes without seeing them incorporated in actual people. How else can they know them? Co-operation, integrity, saintliness, gaiety, all come to have meaning and example for us only as we see them manifested and incarnated in men and women.

The educative power of a group is likely to be proportionate in its real influence to the depth at which the child really belongs to it. One can belong to a group at different levels and it is easy to mistake the depths at which one is really a member of it. A boy of ten who identifies himself with his gang and joins in most of its exploits will only in rare cases have committed more than a superficial part of his personality to membership in it. He belongs to his family in a very different meaning of the verb; he may never be conscious how deeply.

To become a fully committed and involved member of a nation, a church, or even a political party must needs be a long and gradual process, much of which goes on unconsciously at every stage, even though conscious acts of identification and acceptance must also take place. It is certainly possible to be starved of belonging, to fail to be nourished by coming really to belong to anything or anybody. A school to which no one can belong save in a meagre sense of the word can never be a really potent educational medium. If school boards and authorities which employ teachers realized this more surely there might be less frequent transfers of staff from one school to another at short notice and with little consultation. In his autobiography, John Middleton Murry, the distinguished literary critic, tells of passing from a London Board School as a boy of eleven to Christ's Hospital: school ceased to be an external affair for him; he suddenly found himself endowed with ancestors and part of a community. The atmosphere and power of a school is made up from many elements but mostly from the sheer belief of people in its past or its future or in both.

One of the main functions of any school is quite rightly and inevitably a conservative function. If it tries to change the attitudes or the traditions of behaving or thinking of its inhabitants too rapidly or too tendentiously it will succeed only in causing more of their real education to be got from other quarters. For at any time a school is only one educative factor in the lives of its pupils. How much it really matters in shaping, disciplining and energizing the life of a boy or girl will undoubtedly vary from individual to individual. Some will get from home and church and street and friends what others may get from master or mistress, from subjects and books.

A school is likely to influence the majority of its boys or girls most powerfully if its influence is at least not contradictory to trends approved by the parents of its pupils, even if those trends do not actually reflect the parents' own behaviour, religion, morals or speech. Mr. and Mrs. Smith may themselves talk with a Lancashire accent but they are more likely to wish their son or daughter to go to an independent school in another part of England if at heart they feel that it would be a good rather than a bad thing for their offspring to speak with a less local label. An attitude of consent on the part of his parents must indeed be present if the child is to grow up without conflict within an independent school tradition. In America it is the ambition of some families to send their sons to one of the famous preparatory schools in New England. But a boy at one of these schools whose parents believed its social influence harmful or unfortunate could hardly escape internal repression and disturbance.

We probably still underestimate the importance of carrying parents actively with us in assigning John or Mary to this school tradition or that; or in trying to change the temper or ideals of a particular school. There are many boys and girls who would work much harder and do much better in high school if there were more wish and will on the part of their homes and suburbs, and therefore of themselves, that they should do so. Many boys and girls remain passengers in school not so much because of too low an intelligence quotient as because they fail to see the relevance for them of what they are supposed to be learning. We may call them "unacademic" in type. But that in many cases is a description of the effect, not an explanation of the cause. They never really feel that they "belong" and though skilful teacher-technicians may add a good deal of information to their minds in the course of the years, they may never really have had a high school education in anything like a full sense by the time they graduate, nor really have been disciplined by the subjects they have so painfully been first learning and then forgetting.

One of the most urgent needs in education in many Western countries is a much more whole-hearted effort to secure closer understanding between home and school. Speech days and parent-teacher associations can do something, and understanding of the different viewpoints of home and classroom is certainly fostered by them. But a much more individual and intimate contact is needed. As with so much else in education, personal relationships matter most. An approachable principal or class-teacher can help simply by being approachable. The school can sometimes learn from the home as well as the home from the school. The wording of written communications from school to home can be chilling or on the other hand encouraging to the right kind of further contact. In some countries there is a specially trained member of the staff of a school, part of whose time is given to visiting the homes of children whose parents would otherwise remain cut off from the school and from all knowledge of what it was trying to do for their children.

2

We shall misconceive the nature and underestimate the importance of the "discipline" given by a home or church or school if we think of it as concerned merely with behaviour. Only part of the discipline given by the school comes through the study of a particular set of subjects, through the punishments administered or even the qualities and performances which are praised. The discipline it administers is much more subtle and complex in its nature: its origin is to be found in the beliefs, the standards, the faith in a purpose or no-purpose, which live, many of them unconsciously, in the minds of principal and staff and parents, and in the larger society around, which "accepts" the school and allows it to continue. The process of being disciplined is a process of having principles worked into one's character. And the product of discipline, in the sense in which the term is here used, is not simply behaviour but something more basic and primary: it is concerned with the ordering of feeling as well as conduct, with modifying what we want to do, not merely what we do. In this way it is a permission, not a proscription only—a permission to be free men within the tradition of feeling and of culture we are inhabiting.

Discipline, thus, has to do essentially not only with the teaching of conduct or knowledge but with the shaping of attitudes. "Alas!" wrote Coleridge over a century ago, "how many examples are now present to my memory of young men the most anxiously and expensively be-schoolmastered, be-tutored, be-lectured, any thing but *educated;* who have received arms and ammunition instead of skill, strength and courage." It matters immensely to the education of the growing boy or girl what underlying philosophies of life and of education have been taken for granted by the sections of society of which they are members, and by their teachers. For a really accepted philosophy or faith disciplines the inward spirit and for that very reason inevitably comes to affect outward behaviour in its turn.

There is real need that schools should show that they value enthusiasm, insight, sensitivity and faith, and not regard it as their job only to pass on knowledge, however efficiently, or to teach children how to analyze their world —important though that is. If a school succeeds in giving a strong sense to its children of the variety, interest and worth of life it will be doing work greatly needed in our time. A good many schools are better at educating attitudes of detached, unemotional enquiry, of maintained hard work, of energetic, courageous playing of games in teams, than at educating attitudes which involve passiveness, absorption and inward activity rather than effort and outward action. Yet these also are attitudes within the great tradition of Western civilization. They too are deeply social and indispensable to the nourishment and development of individuality. Praying and loving and imagining are as necessary to the good life as memorizing and thinking and striving. It is easy to know too much and feel too little, and because of that to be content to grow up passive in regard to what is important, though in small matters endlessly and restlessly active.

An essential part of education is giving people encouragement, and courage, to believe. And yet, in the mid-twentieth century, as Professor Polanyi of Manchester University has pointed out, "the critical imperative of rejecting any belief that can quite conceivably be doubted has become second nature to us." Perhaps, indeed, you can educate to any depth, whether in home or church or school, *only* people who bring with them a capacity for wonder and belief as well as comprehension, who give themselves; and perhaps good teaching is the sort of teaching which helps people to give themselves at deep levels, so that then they can learn at deep levels too. That can hardly be done by the teacher who is shallow himself, who has no real beliefs or convictions. The sort of education we need is not the sort which will be content only to teach people how to do things, in the sense of instructing them. At all ages education has to be more than an acquisition of accomplishments. In Ivy Compton-Burnett's novel *Daughters and Sons*, Clare remarks somewhere: "Training of that kind doesn't alter people," to which Hetta replies, "It hides them, shall we say? so that it seems to alter them." Education that hides can never be an important sort of education. Real education must compel the exercise of memory and thought but, from time to time, must penetrate deep into feelings too.

Again and again what counts in education is the learner's recognition—it may be subconscious but nevertheless sure—that the knowledge and the tastes and the standards he is being taught really matter to someone's heart. It may be that the reason why so many boys and girls forget so easily the "religious knowledge" they have been taught is that it was taught them with such little passion of belief.

It is difficult to overestimate the importance of really personal contacts in education, for they are the link by which the individual is joined as by an umbilical cord to his social heritage. The more really intimate and personal the contact, the greater the power of education made possible. The mother, who is nature's first and chief educator, is immensely powerful as a teacher because of her closeness to the child. Relationships between people are very much more important than perfection of classroom conditions, a liberal supply of apparatus, a gliding blackboard on rollers, or even comfort. If relationships are right it is possible for children, like grown-ups, to endure hardships and discomforts which might appear crippling. A teacher who can be in real touch with children—whether he is often gruff, bad-tempered and forbidding or mild-tempered, gracious and charming—is likely to be far more influential within them than a more technically efficient instructor who hardly includes their humanity within his interest.

The harsh disciplinarian—whether father or teacher—is not necessarily a powerful disciplinarian at all; often indeed he prevents an inward learning of the discipline by alienating and armouring the child who is being outwardly punished. In these days physically harsh punishment is more rarely administered than it used to be, though the amount still going on may easily be underestimated. For the most part, however, child and parent, teacher and pupil, have come nearer together (as have also characters in novels and plays to their audiences and readers), and so discipline is conveyed in forms that are more subtle and more intimate (as in plays the characters now usually speak prose and but rarely speak loudly).

It is a mistake to imagine that the members of a school staff are even approximately equal in their influence upon their pupils. One teacher who passionately cares for his subject or for his children will have far more influence than five or six who are merely professionals. A teacher who is to make close contact with a child must at times mean intensely what he says and what he does. Intensity indeed is one of the great secrets of teaching. Consider, for example, this account of an early lesson in accuracy: "The teacher gave me a new piece of paper and watched me make my first fold—whereupon she remarked with emotion that I must bring my corners *much* nearer together, and, at the same time, showed me the possibility of this. A new idea of accuracy dawned upon me, and my astonishment was only exceeded by my delight in the marked improvement of my results." [1] Here is discipline in action.

It is, of course, true that on occasion children must be treated as objects—must be prevented, by force if necessary, from playing with matches in a woodshed. Even grown-ups

[1] Joseph Wicksteed, *The Challenge of Childhood*.

may have to be prevented by penalties from crossing a busy street at an intersection except when the green light says "Yes." Commands of this sort backed by sanctions are justified on the simple principle that they physically save life. But such prohibitions have little to do with education at the deeper levels. Good teaching is teaching that raises the interest, the imagination, the energies of the child and makes use of them. It is teaching which makes him more fully human. But is it not true that some of our teaching is more successful at getting people to act at being instead of really being—to act at being knowledgeable, to act at being citizens, even to act at enjoying themselves?

> "She gave me eyes, she gave me ears,
>   And humble cares, and delicate fears,"

says Wordsworth of his sister Dorothy. The same sort of thing is true of very much good teaching: there is something about it of admitting people a little further into membership of humanity. The eyes and ears and fears it gives us are those of a whole gathering of feeling and thinking men and women, present, past and to come. On the other hand, the bad teacher only too often substitutes something very like propaganda for education. When the class are absorbed in, say, *The Passing of Arthur*, intensely disciplined in imagination by their actual experiencing of what is being read, he may suddenly break off reading and say: "John, sit up straight. Robert, stop playing with that paper clip—and all of you—yes, *all* of you, I said—pay attention to the onomatopeia in line 86. If you don't concentrate, you won't pass the final examination."

Such a teacher is indulging in superficial propaganda for self-interested purposes. And the process is apt to be anti-educative. He is doing what he can to prevent his pupils from becoming fully human, and from exercising their humanity.

Some of the deepest impressions of all are those which pierce silently down into the mind—and reach places where the secret seeds of life lie hid. In our schools are we not tempted sometimes to overestimate the importance of an ability to produce, almost on demand, knowledge and information at conscious levels? Some of the most important truths, as Edmond Holmes, the author of *What Is and What Might Be*, pointed out long ago, are truths which ascend quite gradually to conscious levels and are only ready to give themselves off in the form of information a long while after the experience itself has been received. Too constant a succession of examinations in this subject and that is a frequent cause of superficiality. Mere busyness is not educative; Satan finds some mischief still for busy hands to do—and the mischief can be subtle mischief: a starving of sensibility and imagination. It is necessary at all stages in life to give people peace in which to grow; that may not always mean absence of noise or of things happening, but absence of demand that they should have urgently to delve up from the mind now this, now that bit of what lies buried. There is need in life from time to time of a "creative pause" and that is true of children at least as much as of older people.

It is often forgotten that though forty boys and girls sitting in a classroom may be receptacles of exactly the same words from their teacher during a given school hour, each nevertheless is absorbing from the lesson something different from all the others. And the succession of experiences pouring into the child's mind each day, from out-of-school sources and in-school sources, differs greatly from child to child. It is difficult to understand how some of the experiences and learnings which are absorbed make their contribution to unified selfhood. But we must have faith. As Wordsworth exclaims:

> "Ah me! that all
> The terrors, all the early miseries,
> Regrets, vexations, lassitudes, that all
> The thoughts and feelings which have been infus'd
> Into my mind, should ever have made up
> The calm existence that is mine when I
> Am worthy of myself!"

There is certainly a place for competition in the school, but parent or teacher must be careful not to foster rivalry almost as an end in itself. For one thing such competitiveness is likely to substitute information for knowledge on many occasions because it concentrates the mind too externally on the subject being studied. We ought also to ask ourselves seriously, if we are tempted to appeal to the competitive instinct as a standard tactic, whether it is really a stimulant which ought to be indulged in *ad lib.* by anybody; for its logical aim at the final stage is isolation, so that the conqueror may be alone at the top. But if we are living a civilized life such aggression is not often called for; and a society run on savagely competitive lines is not the best fitted for producing lives to be lived with quality.

In schools that are co-educational it is a common and

convenient practice to urge the boys to compete against the girls in this subject or that, and this no doubt is sometimes an easy way of securing a zestful classroom. But a standard reliance upon this technique is really quite incompatible with the underlying aims of co-education, or indeed of wise education for either sex. The point of the co-educational school is to help the boys and girls in it to know that their similarities as human beings are incomparably more important than their differences, intriguing and interesting and exciting though those differences are. If we believe in co-education—and there are many powerful arguments against as well as for it—one reason is that we recognize that in grown-up society co-operation between the sexes is natural and essential. There are tendencies in Western society which tempt us to exaggerate the differences between boys and girls, or men and women, rather than to underestimate them. Advertisers, journalists and salesmen of many varieties find the stimulations of sex-rivalry and sex-differentiation a way towards the achievement of their own ends. The fact is that there are important and indispensable "feminine" elements present in every boy and powerful "masculine" impulses in every girl. Co-education has to go on *inside* all our pupils if they are to be educated so that they remain unified. The justification of co-education is that it may help to bring out in boys and girls alike both the masculine and the feminine qualities necessary to full humanity. And to encourage competition too often simply on a principle of sex-difference is, to say the least, unthoughtful.

In any school it is important to arrange for many situations in which competition between individuals is difficult.

In the normal everyday work in any subject opportunities arise for group activity, not merely with the competitive end in mind of setting group against group, but partly for the value of relationships which are brought into being when people are working in unity for a common purpose: for example, in the writing or acting of a play, in making a survey of a village or suburb, in planning a tour of some unknown region. There is need for wider groupings sometimes than can be found from pupils all of the same age. The students in the twelfth grade ought at times to be seeing their responsibility for the ninth graders as something other than hoping they behave themselves in the corridors. And youngsters in the ninth grade ought to know the boys and girls in the twelfth as people, not only as heroes of the football field. This friendly relationship is certainly more common in the States than it is in England.

But to imagine that freedom comes from "self-expression" at any superficial level is to deceive ourselves. Our aim must be so to educate boys and girls that they will have the best chance of "fitting in" to their society and yet have their capacity for spontaneity preserved. By their upbringing they must be made into members of their community, at first unnoticeably but more and more with their own co-operation. Such an upbringing is authoritative in that it makes it difficult for them to be content to be superficial or superficially self-expressive, but natural and as easy as possible for them on occasion to feel with genuineness, to think and act at a personal level.

The key problem in educating any society is to get people to want things enough. That is a task for the imaginative statesman, the lively, patient teacher. But, even for them, it is only possible to get boys and girls, or men and women, to want the things they are nearly ready to want. However anxious we may be to educate for individuality and high attainment, all education essentially involves trusting tradition, trusting communal wisdom and allowing environment and social habit to build the channels through which the vital currents will flow. And such trust has more to justify it than a hasty judgment might think. We have to trust the organic workings of our bodily functions, for we cannot do much else for most of our time; we have to take for granted and make use of the social organism around us. The education of the unconscious mind, of habit and attitude, matters a very great deal. The individual learns the communal wisdom through persons who deeply incorporate it and convey it to him.

3

But developing individuality means also developing in consciousness of self and developing in will. A mouse grows rapidly and quite unconsciously into a fully mature mouse; but a man cannot reach full maturity without a concept of what he ought to be and do, and an active will to realize that concept. In other words, it is essential for a person who is to develop much real individuality to become able, from time to time, to look at himself from the outside. It is often only possible to discover what one's motives are by observing one's own conduct and reflecting upon it; and adolescence is the period when this self-examination is beginning. Some of the awkwardnesses and uncertainties of the adolescent arise because he is not sure where the frontiers of his personality end, or how he is to develop his own individuality. He plays at being a number of attractive and maybe wayward people other than himself and perhaps passes through a phase of loving to dress up and of loving ritual. He tries to find individuality by going widely afield for it or by playing someone else's part for a while. But the most promising direction he must eventually find within. It is important not to be afraid of the introspectiveness of adolescence, for introspection is indispensable to mature adulthood.

The problem is to ensure a real membership, and recognition of membership, of one's society, and at the same time grow to be a person with an independent will and centre. It is by no accident that the words "will and centre" come together here. For "will" as the term is now used is very central in life. To have will in this sense means having a policy, so that when a conscious decision is called for between two possible courses of action character is expressed in the choice that is made. It may not be— it rarely is—possible to see all the consequences of such a choice, but one accepts the consequences in advance, both those which can be seen and those which cannot.

The training of will is not a training of a "faculty." A great deal of practice in showing determination on the football field, and taking many rapid decisions there with mind and body in close co-operation, does not necessarily train a man to be strong-willed in a bar after the game. A strong will to succeed in business may not be at a man's service when it comes to climbing a mountain in the holidays. Certainly a child must come to know his power to control himself and must come to feel that, though this power is difficult to wield, it is good to wield it. But all these are not enough. Building up the volitional structure so that action may conform to insight is not a simple business of educating a strong will and then of spreading it out to cover life-situations in great variety. To have will power of the essential kind means coming to take personal responsibility for the direction of progress of one's society too. The education of such a sense of responsibility as this must needs be a long business.

In school, one way of educating a sense of responsibility is through giving boys and girls duties to do that are real duties, so that they learn how to pour themselves into being really proctors or monitors, into being really responsible for the production of a magazine or some part of it, the very reputation of the school being risked in the process. Expectations can be potent means of educating: what we expect of others, and what they know we expect of them. It is difficult to ensure that all the children in a class are given as much responsibility as they can properly take. Teachers—and parents too—are likely to underestimate the amount of responsibility which children of twelve, fourteen, sixteen can bear (if they do it occasionally) without strain and to the great nourishment of individuality and will. To have to take responsibility and to develop sensitiveness to situations is a creator of standards and of really personal convictions, for standards and convictions are first-cousins. We want boys and girls to achieve on the one hand a real independence and on the other standards of thought and of conduct that are personal and sincere.

A person who is to retain individuality over a long period must also remain at unity with himself. The retention of self-unity, as Wordsworth saw so clearly, is helped most by the ability to recollect at all stages of life one's own past and the experiences which have mattered in one's development. We pay a great deal of attention in schools to having children memorize facts and passages of verse and even prose. But at least equally important is a training of ability to recollect moods and past experiences. This capacity is difficult to train because it is so much less within the teacher's knowledge and because classes in any case are so big. But to be able to recollect at will one's own childhood and growth can be a great bulwark of individuality; and a great help too in enabling people to catch up with themselves and so to be really unified at any given time. It is, as a matter of fact, the state of not being able to catch up with oneself that is so often called immaturity. As any man looks back over life, it is clearer than ever that many of the most important things for him were ones which happened to him and within him: they were not achievements.

Unless the growing child draws from roots deep in his society, he will remain unnourished and unable to make a contribution to it. Unless he can feel and speak and act from "within normality" people will not hear or be able to understand what he says. The languages we speak must, in fact, have much in common with those other people speak if other people are going to listen to what we say. The pure individualist, if there could be such a person, would live in a vacuum; he would be a Robinson Crusoe with not even a Friday to influence or convert. In any society men will be able to be individual only in certain ways and directions. If we seek to foster individuality as an end in itself we shall run the risk of producing simply oddity. Real individuality is the result of much living and experiencing within a society, or a significant part of it, and then of letting experience come up to consciousness. The good teacher has often to know when not to interfere, when not to dig up, when not to examine. It is the organic which grows; the inorganic does not.

In brief, if we are to educate men of vision and a sense of responsibility, environment will be one of our chief instruments—and a permeating environment made up not of streets and buildings but of people. For the transfer of tradition and purpose which we have called discipline will not be the foe of individuality but the preventive of kinds of individuality which have no long significance and are expressions only of the superficial. Unless one learns really to belong to humanity, there will be no possibility of so communicating truths to others that they will be able either to apprehend or to comprehend one's meaning.

6

THE SCHOOL AND ITS CURRICULUM

1

Any school has to do its work within a particular society, and quite inevitably it will take for granted, unexamined, many of the traditional concepts of what a school should be which its principal and his assistants have inherited. But scratch an opinion and find a value. Its curriculum, the proportions of time it gives to the various subjects chosen, the rules to which it adheres, its belief in the educative value of playing baseball or football, the importance it attaches to good speech, will largely have been determined by a series of value-judgments that are for the most part unconscious. If the school is to do more to train insight, to foster depth and a sense of purpose in its children, in what ways may its curriculum need to be modified?

The main tradition of education whether in England

or America has, of course, never been concerned with a narrow academic achievement as the one important thing. In England the old boy who comes back on Speech Day to dilate upon the need for "character" and to point his finger at the connection between education and character-building is a figure with a whole receding file of grandfathers at his back, dating at any rate to the days of William of Wykeham, whose notion when he founded his College of St. Mary at Winchester in 1382 was that the formation of character and of "manners" went hand in hand with sound learning. The corporate life of the school, he thought, would help to make men. And it is significant that most English grammar schools founded between the fourteenth and the sixteenth centuries, like most of the schools which grew up in the villages in seventeenth- and eighteenth-century England to give a primary education, and about which we are finding out more every year, were established on a religious foundation. However much grammar schools and choir schools in actual practice may have been for a great part of their time establishments for hammering the rudiments of Latin and Greek grammar, and of mathematics, not without cruelty and pain into the heads of their pupils, there was the link with religion and the sung services of the Church—with, that is, deep ways of expressing insight and feeling, hope and desire, both conscious and unconscious.

Traditionally, too, English schooling has for long given an important place to games and sports which demand health and purpose and will, at least within a certain range. It is still taken for granted, however surprisingly, that there should be a games afternoon at least once a week even in a grammar school which prepares children in the most cut-throat way for competitive scholarship and other examinations preliminary to university entrance. No laboratories on Wednesday afternoons is still the acknowledged law in the "Redbrick" or modern universities; and no lectures between lunch and tea-time remains the rule at Oxbridge. The continental visitor is puzzled—and so also is the Hindu, who has known no change of this sort from his academic labours.

In American public schools, although there is immense emphasis on sports and physical education and real belief in training courtesy, friendliness and ease in human relationships, there has come a break with religious observance that is almost complete. The fundamental cause for this has been the widely felt need for non-sectarianism in the interest of national unity rather than an opposition to religion itself or to the worship of God at proper times or in proper places.

In America and England alike, however, the curriculum does far less than it might to educate "the feeling intellect" and a deeply personal sense of values. It is especially important today that the reason—which includes faith and a humble sense of the mystery of things—should be educated as well as the intelligence, important though intelligence is. "Reason," says Jaspers, "is never without intelligence, but it is infinitely more than intelligence . . . It relates all the various meanings of truth to one another, by asserting each one." It is not indeed improbable that the content of what is called "general intelligence" in any society is affected by what that society values as intelligent. Some of the special isolates—musical ability and manual ability, for example—

may in fact be regarded as special because they are less valued as evidences of what is looked upon as intelligence in that civilization. Not to educate the intelligence strenuously is to produce disunity and inhumanity in those who are growing up; and the more intelligent the child, the greater the danger of disunity. Nevertheless a man is more than his intellectual capacities. For certain purposes—assigning, for example, a boy or girl to the type of secondary education most suited to his abilities—it is useful to be able to measure a person's "intellectual capacity," even if we may not be exactly sure what it is that we are measuring. But we must beware of assuming that intelligence tests in their present form tell us more than a limited amount about the more hidden potentialities of one human mind compared with another.

An aspect of mental functioning on which intelligence tests shed comparatively little light as yet is, as Professor D. W. Harding of Bedford College, London, says, "the relation between the highly differentiated cognitive surface of the mind—solving its straightforward problems with precise words and numbers or clearly organized spatial designs and cubes—and the much less manageable aspects of the personality where interest, sentiment, desire, mood and attitude are in a fluid condition . . . The simple (and for a time doubtless useful) device of psychologists was the fiction that intelligence could be clearly distinguished from the emotional and conative aspects of the mind, and dealt with separately. There are plenty of signs that that fiction is being abandoned." [1] It may indeed be that the heartless intellectual is not even as deeply intelli-

[1] *The Use of English*, Vol. 2, No. 3, p. 144.

gent as he imagines. For capacities for some very important kinds of knowing may be lacking in him.

2

By far the most important factor in producing through the
school a more human comprehension in children, and a
more lively sense of purpose, is the quality and outlook
of the teacher himself. That is why the selection and education of teachers are of such key importance in the whole
field of education. Provided that one has teachers of quality, the particular subjects chosen for inclusion in the curriculum matter rather less than is sometimes supposed.
It is possible to teach the same fundamentals through a
wide variety of subjects—though no doubt some subjects
lend themselves much more easily than others to particular aspects of the whole task. It is difficult, however, to see
why specialization in a comparatively few subjects should
be educatively undesirable from the age of fourteen or so
—provided that those subjects are taught so that each includes a wide range of interest and ministers to the needs
of the child and of the time in which he is living. Much
will depend upon the background of the teacher. But a
"general" education consisting of a number of subjects
each taught in a narrowly specialist way can certainly fail
to be humanizing, and three or four specialisms so taught
that life comes through them may yield an education that
is generous and humane. "Each specialism no doubt has its
bottleneck and some never get so far as to reach it," says
Professor John F. Danby of the University of Wales. "But

those who do, and are carried through it, come to a realization of some of the other knowledges their specialization needs in order to know itself: and this kind of liberal education only specialization can give . . . A superficial coursing round the rim of the curriculum is no substitute for progress along the spokes towards the centre." The deeper educative value of any subject is not to be found in a mere knowledge of the facts or a mere attainment of the skills it imparts.

We chase far too readily a will-o'-the-wisp called "a certain minimum knowledge which every boy and girl should possess by the time he leaves school," forgetting that the test is not what he possesses—in some sense of the word—when he is examined in it at sixteen or eighteen, but what he possesses twenty or thirty years after the day he left school behind. Has he got from his school days a sense of life's importance, an inkling that maintained, disciplined enthusiasms matter, that imagination, sensibility and depth are of greater value than wide information, that books ought to be used and read all through life, that "happiness" is not the goal?

By and large, secondary schools, whether public or private, commercial or college preparatory, have not been bold enough in omission. For some pupils, arithmetic and mathematics might be entirely dropped at fourteen with great gain to the time available for other things and with no loss to the effective, useful knowledge they would have later in life. For other children who have been learning a foreign language, whether ancient or modern, or drawing, or woodwork, not too profitably for three or four years, it would be well to stop teaching these subjects at fourteen or fifteen and make room for others which in their case might be of greater value.

Our first aim must be to encourage and maintain the child's vitality, for without vitality neither width nor depth of learning will be possible. To do this is in part a physical matter, in part a mental. For all but rare temperaments, maintenance of energy, strength of character, delicacy of perception, clarity of judgment all depend upon a continuing flow of vitality. Believing, as they so rightly do, in the importance of exercise it is surprising that some schools are still comparatively uninterested in the sheer importance of posture, of learning how to breathe aright, how to relax at will with some thoroughness, the importance of diet in the lunches provided by the school and therefore under its control. The basic framework of the action-system of all vertebrates is posture. The finer and subtler patterns of behaviour are grafted on to postural positions and postural attitudes. It is not simply chance which causes confidence and an upright stance to tend to go together and to react upon each other; or lack of confidence and a stoop. Physiotherapy can in itself help to bring about a psychotherapy, building up in the emotional organization feeling-attitudes to correspond with the attitudes of body. There is much evidence to show that the acquisition of techniques both of deep breathing and of ability to relax can be immensely helpful in the preservation or restoration of vitality. To learn to impose calmness on the body is one way of learning how to impose calmness on the mind. But normally little effort is made to teach these techniques adequately or to keep them in a state of preservation.

The amount of exercise needed by different people of course varies a great deal. Too much can be as harmful to vitality as too little—and the intensity with which exercise is taken can be too great as well as too small. The variety, interest and opportunity for individual thought and action in modern physical education work help to make it effective for the preservation of vitality. In some people music produces a relaxation of mind which can greatly aid the flow of bodily energy and impulse. One cannot but feel that more use than is habitual might be made by many schools both of music and the bodily interpretation of music in their physical education syllabus.

As we have suggested, the actual subjects for the schools to teach may vary a good deal and still comprise a selection of high potential educationally. Not only the existence, but the content and intimate emphases of a school "subject," have their origins in the society outside the school. The continued evolution and fashioning of the curriculum and the acceptance in any age of that curriculum by teachers, parents and employers have in part social explanations. What is effectively and permanently absorbed and learnt is apt to be determined by the social values and implicit value-judgments of the nation, the age, the group to which the learner belongs—expressed through the rewards subtly given by society to what is approved as "normal" or "good." Thus it was easier to learn to be a fervent imperialist in the England of 1900 than in the England of 1950. Research into the nature and extent of the approval given by different social groupings to various pieces of learning would throw a good deal of light upon the reasons for differing degrees of success in teaching them. The learning of facts and techniques and skills is often an indication of the effectiveness with which attitudes of mind and particular ways of feeling have already been learnt. In some schools it is probably much harder to teach art, or French, or chess, or music, than in other schools taking pupils of equal intelligence. The effect of the real (often unconscious) wishes of parents and of surrounding society upon the directions in which learning is easily possible is a major subject for investigation.

What can be taught "through" science now includes a great deal which once might have been taught appropriately through Latin; geography in one school can be shaped so that it becomes the vehicle of a number of the disciplines conveyed through social studies or English or science in another school. Much of the effectiveness of any subject in the education of those who study it depends upon the keenness and depth of the interest aroused in them; and, as any teacher knows, the interest of the surrounding society in a particular field is of the greatest help in causing it to be educatively valuable at a particular period. In all education, as Whitehead has penetratingly remarked, the main cause of failure is staleness. A teacher to whom almost any topic is fresh and living in its interest can educate boys and girls or men and women through that topic.

Moreover the content of subjects called by the same name at different periods and in different countries, and different universities and schools in the same country, can be so different in range that we can easily be deceived into thinking that the name defines the subject-area instead of being merely the label on the bottle. It is illuminating, for example, to compare the extremely varied content of the syllabuses in different British universities at the present time all leading in three years to an Honours degree in German.

Nevertheless it is important that during his school life the child should on the one hand be given—whatever the subjects he studies—the tools he needs in the form of acquired habit, skill and factual information to support himself within the society of which he is a member and to live without waste of energy in fruitless conflicts; and on the other hand that he should be nourished and vitalized in spirit so that he is enabled to live authentically and with a purpose.

A large part of schooling must inevitably be occupied in imparting indispensable technical knowledge and essential practical skills. And this will be so whether we are thinking of the manual labourer brought up in an area full of traffic, blunt speech and workers' loyalties, or of a highly individual, self-contained scientist or administrator planning the means by which society itself is to be controlled and preserved. A great proportion of human life must quite unavoidably be taken up with utilitarian concerns—not merely with sleeping, with the growing, preparing and eating of food, but with safeguarding the interests of the community and with learning and applying knowledge which will maintain and advance the community's safety and stability, its health and prosperity. The soldier, the doctor, the engineer, the chemist in his laboratory and the salesman are alike concerned for much of their time to ensure that life goes on or goes forward "on the level," yielding incidentally its dividends of satisfaction, contentment and perhaps happiness.

Yet happiness varies not only in amount but in depth; nor are perceptions and intuitions that there is "meaning" in life to be gainsaid even though their coming may be momentary and not easily to be resurrected. The knowledge brought in by the senses and the feelings: by listening to music, by reading novels, by human love, suffering, religious experience, humour and sympathy, is not to be denied or disproved, even though one's neighbours may not be sharing the same knowledge at the same time, and may never come to possess knowledge which is exactly identical. The acquisition of any number of facts will not in itself breed an awareness either of mystery or meaning in life. And such awareness is indispensable if we are to educate vision as well as intelligence.

A very considerable range of the subjects it is possible to teach in school can be taught so that they train now what may be called "narrow" attention and now what may be called "wide." The exercise of both kinds of attention is important to living a good life. Observation is a tense activity, what Ernst Junger meant when he called seeing "an act of aggression." It involves a concentrated, narrow attention. Contemplation, on the other hand, involves looking: that is, opening one's eyes receptively to whatever offers itself to one's vision, with experiences allowed to enter in.[2]

In the past the two subjects most used for training narrow attention were Latin and mathematics. It is possible to

[2] Cf. Joseph Pieper, *Leisure, the Basis of Culture.*

arrange their content without too much difficulty so that they can be taught with little room for vagueness and uncertainty. When a sentence is studied with the concentration focused upon it, it can be construed and its import made logically clear. When an equation is solved it is solved and the process can be proved. In Latin and mathematics it is always possible to set the pupil something to do which is just within his reach. Each of these subjects can in fact be kept beautifully under control and its content imparted step by step, stage by stage, according to the pupil's capacities and knowledge. Both Latin and mathematics, however, can be used to some extent in the training of wider attention—Latin because it is a language in which a cultured literature is written; and mathematics because it is a language of symbol with its own long history of development and a revelation of a self-contained imaginative world almost infinite in extent and scope. But at the more elementary stages both Latin and mathematics appear more suitable for the discipline of narrow attention than wide.

The physical sciences, the social studies, American history, geography, modern foreign languages and English can all be so taught that they too chiefly involve exact, "narrow" observation. If they are to act as disciplines of this sort, their subject-matter must be more consciously and carefully arranged for the purpose than is the case with Latin or mathematics; and the composition of examination papers in them will be a highly skilful and technical occupation. During this century great progress has been made in making possible their use as disciplines of this kind. But it is easy in such re-planning and adaptation of the subject to lessen—almost without noticing that we have done so—its ability to educate wider attention, to deepen human understanding or to feed contemplation. The tendency is, as it were, to make every subject more extroverted while bringing it more under control. Almost every book read during school hours becomes a textbook or a reference book; there are well-compiled tests and examination papers to be taken at thoughtfully adapted intervals; the travel approach to geography gives place to a much more ordered and active study of causes and effects. I would not for a moment question the greatly increased efficiency of almost every subject taught along modern lines to keep the child's attention and intriguingly compel his interest in it to continue. But in this very admirable process we tend to have forgotten that there are nourishing kinds of relaxation as well as ones which are a waste of time. We make a mistake about human nature if we think of it as needing simply "play" and "work": there are many kinds of play, many kinds of work, many kinds of attention. "Work hard, play hard" is a deceptive maxim and a gross oversimplification of what is really wise. To teach any subject as a formulation of fact or knowledge, rather than as an approach to life and truth under one aspect, is tempting and not overdifficult.

This is one of the reasons why the teaching of science, even with close attention to a good textbook, sometimes fails to convey to the learner much of the scientific attitude. It is, of course, easier to treat the teaching of science as a separate teaching of knowledge about chemistry, knowledge about physics, or knowledge about biology, than to teach all three so that they are seen—and felt—as parallel approaches to the study of life and matter. Many of the advances now being made in scientific knowledge are being made in territories where these separate "subjects" overlap; and it is of high importance that in our science teaching we should convey the idea that the scientific attitude is one which yields every month more and more knowledge, some. of it with far-reaching consequences to the outlook for mankind.

In our own day it is especially important that much effort should go into discussing the limitations of the relevance of the scientific attitude. "Its range of application," says one book upon teaching well-known in England, and published a few years ago, "is unlimited." [3] By no means. In a very pointed and penetrating essay Mr. A. R. Bielby, Principal of Huddersfield College, has shown the practical difficulties of so teaching science that it develops maturity and reverence in those who are taught. It can be taught so that it ministers to "cosmic piety" or so that it is an introduction only to the exploitation of the universe by man. To Kepler, 350 years ago, science was "thinking God's thoughts after him." "The chief aim of all investigation of the external world," said Kepler in the early seventeenth century, "should be to discover the rational order and harmony which have been impressed on it by God." "Science," says J. D. Bernal in the mid-twentieth century, "is the means of obtaining practical mastery over nature by understanding it."

Mr. Bielby draws a picture of a more or less typical sixth-form science specialist in an ordinary English gram-

[6] Council for Curriculum Reform. *The Content of Education*, p. 146.

mar school today. But the parallel is close with that of many a boy in the twelfth grade at an American high school. "He is probably the son of an artisan, from a good home but with little background of culture, in a school where fee-payers, who bring with them a more leisured attitude, are not allowed. He has an eye on the main end, examination success, for he depends on scholarships, and the standards are high. Success means economic security and social position. It is a matter of being conducted over a prescribed route by forced marches. He has little time, and is too tired, to explore by-roads; he has no choice but to be utilitarian. Yet he needs emotional security and confidence to grow on. Where are these to be found? In the things he can understand and master, the techniques and elegances of his work, for he is uncertain of himself in anything that is personal. He dare not commit himself in the arts, he cannot trust his own judgments in literature, he is acutely aware of his lack of social confidence. The world of values is a world of shades of grey, and he prefers the clear blacks and whites of mathematics. There things are manageable, he knows about them, they give him confidence. Mathematics becomes, in Whitehead's phrase, 'a refuge from the goading urgency of contingent happenings.'

"So he shuns the very things that would enrich him as a person. In self-defence he pretends he does not want them, he has not time for them, they do not minister to his self-confidence. Unconsciously he belittles them till the person he could have been vanishes, and even his science, instead of being a discipline, becomes an end, itself degenerated to a technique, a know-how of getting through examinations and later a know-how of technical processes, and not the beginnings of a philosophy." [4]

But any of the sciences can be taught so that it nourishes imagination and adds to generalizing power. Here are not simply facts and laws to be memorized but the mind of man learning with humility—and flashes of insight—something of the nature of things, not simply so that he can put his knowledge to material use and make conquests of space and disease, though there is wonder in that, but so that he can know his power and realize his limitations. And there are many imaginative scientists who have a philosophy of science as well as an immense range of scientific knowledge. They are aware that the scientific attitude is objective and self-critical, a sharp and powerful instrument of the human mind, serving its master from period to period. "Scientific truth," says C. A. Coulson, Professor of Applied Mathematics at Oxford, "is dependent on, and influenced by, changing standards and judgments and developing criteria. That leads us to suppose that truth is something experienced rather than discovered; and that it is in the experiencing that its significance lies." [5]

What matters is that the child should learn to value, and sometimes himself to share, the scientist's foresight, patience, and planning; the sternness and strictness of the degree of accuracy to which he works; his willingness to be controlled by truth. Reverence for objective fact and respect for the working of natural law are parts of the discipline which it is essential that any good education

[4] *Researches and Studies*, Number 7, p. 45.
[5] *Question*, Vol. 6, No. 1, pp. 44-5.

should give. "Things are what they are and their consequences will be what they will be." It is a very inadequate
understanding of science which leads people to assume
that its concern is merely with inventing and arranging
things for the wealth and comfort of mankind. The danger today, however, is not so much that the importance of
science and its applications will fail to be seen, or that a
flow of highly trained technicians will not be forthcoming
during the next few generations, but that more inward
and individual growth will be left to wither. It is only too
easy *propter vitam vivendi perdere causas* and to find that
our education is producing more and more perfect autom-
ata, fewer and fewer good men.

7

THE EDUCATION OF UNDERSTANDING

In almost every type of school the years since 1900 have seen a great increase in the amount of knowledge and range of skills which boys and girls leaving at thirteen or fifteen or eighteen were expected to possess. But in general it is true that we have been more successful in fashioning minds able to deal comfortably with material things, skilful within limits in arranging and manipulating, than minds able to use insight and understanding. If people are to develop a personal sense of values, for use at first hand, it can only be by preserving and developing the sensitiveness, the power to feel and understand, which is theirs already in some degree as a birthright. The growth of these capacities to greater maturity is not so much the outcome of concentrating upon particular subjects or making additions to the curriculum as of bringing young people up in an environment in which there are many others who have the attitudes and kinds of sensitiveness we are seeking to foster, an environment in which values are recognized and judgments of value are frequently and naturally made.

People do not learn values simply by being taught about them. One can teach a great deal of truth about values without at all teaching values themselves. "Just as we cannot know music," says W. E. Hocking, the distinguished Harvard philosopher, "by hearing music truly analysed and described, neither can we know anger, joy, forgiveness or loyalty by having any of them demonstrated. These experiences are part of a normal life, and for the most part our treatments of these subjects stop short of demonstration. In brief, values have to be discovered rather than taught. No beginner in life can foresee what values lie ahead of him. He encounters them, as it were, by accident. Each new value is a new surprise. The same is true of the material values, and of the moral and higher values. . . . How from the taste of the apple, or the cherry, or the melon, could one foretell the taste of the mango or the papaya? Each one of these experiences is unique. Similarly with moral values: from the ordinary enjoyments of normal action and sensation, no one could foresee the peculiar satisfaction of overcoming a petty resentment. Value has to be revealed by the turns of experience which come to men individually . . . The achievement is essentially a solitary one, a personal discovery." [1]

To attend to this side of education has not always been regarded as important, or, if important, as properly the business of the school. At a time when most real education

[1] *The Obligation of Universities to the Social Order*, p. 339.

was carried on in the home and the fields and the village community, the part controlled by the school was so small a proportion of the whole that there was no need for it to be so regarded. The child needs plenty of experiences coming into his everyday life—brought by interesting happenings, the learning of new facts, by travel and adventure, by the things he makes and so on; but he also needs continually to be nourished by experiences which come through dealing and communicating with other human beings at many levels, with his feelings involved or likely to be involved. Some of these experiences he can get through reading and listening and looking, many only by drinking life neat.

Activities, craft-work, projects, school gardening, school journeys may all make their contribution to interest and experience. But almost every argument used on behalf of projects and of education through "natural" situations rather than "artificial" subjects applies more forcibly still to the education of the sense of human values. In themselves activities may do little to educate feeling and insight, especially after the pre-adolescent stage has begun; for activities can so easily be full of sound (if not fury) and signify nothing. There is something excessively Western in practical activity as a goal or even as the only means of reaching a goal. It is easy to aim at keeping children or adolescents occupied, whether in youth clubs or in doing plenty of homework; to attach great importance to the quantity of skills acquired, facts memorized, or hours excitingly filled up; to imagine that there is somehow immense virtue in doing for the very sake of avoiding not doing. But however full of fascinating occupations a school may be, the education of power to understand imaginatively is the outcome of dealings with life more intense and subtle still. The attainment of insight and a hierarchy of values personally felt and acknowledged are the greater goals; attainments of technique and of capacity to pass the time enjoyably, lesser ones only.

The thoroughness with which a school teaches its lessons is of prime importance and so is the zest with which it gets boys and girls to work. But thoroughness can be a deceptive term. Knowledge thoroughly learned in an artificial and "schoolly" world, or for examination purposes, may be superficially learned. It may be remembered rather than assimilated. And it may be superficial, one-dimensional knowledge too. It may be left to a very few teachers—often without their being very well aware that it has been so left —to help boys and girls to feel and know the reasonableness of all that part of life that is beyond logic or reasoning. They may be teachers of science, languages or any other subject. But most frequently perhaps they are in these days teachers of English, the arts, music, or, in England, religious knowledge.

> "Full fathom five thy father lies;
>   Of his bones are coral made."

>   "Light thickens, and the crow
>   Makes wing to th' rooky wood."

> "The hornèd Moon, with one bright star
>   Within the nether tip."

The Ancient Mariner judged by most criteria overtly recognized by the contemporary world (though not by our society underneath the surface) is silly stuff, and yet in the

English period it is treated with the utmost normality, as unquestionably the work of a great poet. Judged by any logical mind justly and without prejudice, *Macbeth* and *King Lear* are incredible plays, yet they move and disturb. There is something in a good deal of literature, whether English, Greek, French or Latin, like much of life itself.

The tendency of a number of the subjects as taught to the modern boy or girl at school is to encourage him to think that the objective demonstrable truths of fact are in practice the real, and the only real, truths, or at least a good deal more important than any others. Quite rightly we try to teach him that he must deduce conclusions from given data and not import imaginary data to help him arrive at the conclusions he would like to draw. Facts are sacred, logic is compelling. But there are more things in heaven and earth than facts or logic, and the school is apt to fight too shy of them.

The inward life is a life of imagining and feeling, and upon its health and vigour the quality of our living and the quality of our convictions will depend. If any training of a sense of values, any growth of a deep sense of purpose, is to be possible, children must not lose their power to experience. Subjects which, rightly taught, will help them to keep this power must be significant parts of the curriculum. The indispensable thing to realize about most forms of art is that they convey the experience of man as experience, bringing with them the tang and taste of life, disciplining the attentive spirit by their resolute facing of the ways in which people live and things happen. By this means the spirit is stretched and helped to grow.

It sometimes happens in the secondary school today that

art and music receive scant regard, more especially in those schools which concentrate on preparing students for college or university. Because philosophy itself is fitted only for the study of the adult mind we fail to incorporate within the school curriculum enough philosophical content. In England religious knowledge and science are not usually treated as having a philosophic element within them before the sixth form is reached, if then. And the possibilities of literature as an educator of the imagination, of philosophical interests and of the feelings are not enough realized. Imagination is essentially the power by which we try to apprehend living things in their individuality, not as categories, and as they live and move, not as objects arrested and fixed for methodical study. In this, as Edwin Muir has pointed out, "it is quite different from analytical experiment, which immobilizes and isolates things in order to discover the constituents of which they are made and the laws by which they work. Imagination gives knowledge of things but never exact knowledge, since it cannot and does not wish to study them under a fixed and artificial condition which makes exact knowledge possible. . . . for exact knowledge is only a fragment of the knowledge which we need in order to live a human life."

Literature, religion where it is taught, music and the arts naturally confront the pupil with situations and give him experiences which challenge the idea that a detached, objective attitude is the only right and appropriate one to take up. He may begin to see that some myths are true in another way altogether from the literal, and that the truths they contain cannot be conveyed in the language of a mathematical proof or of a chemical reaction. The typical citizen of our time finds and makes for himself a world much poorer in content than he should. He is interested most of all in the surface of things. He is not a very *experiencing* sort of person and lacks sure standards because his experiencing power has never penetrated down to any elements on which he can stand. One of the most obvious qualities of twentieth-century poetry and prose in Europe is the liveliness of sense of which it gives evidence in its writers. To read them, if our spirits are awake, is to re-inherit a birthright of sense-experiencing. I think, for example, of the novels of Willa Cather, D. H. Lawrence and Joyce Cary, the poems of Robert Frost, T. S. Eliot and Dylan Thomas, the childhood chapters of a remarkable number of autobiographies, such as Sigrid Undset's *The Longest Years*, Alison Uttley's *The Country Child* and Leslie Paul's *The Living Hedge*. But power to experience is not an end in itself, for the most satisfying life is not one merely of sensations. To what do experiences contribute? How are they related to maturity and growth?

The extent to which a man has grown is to be tested by these among other things: (i) the variety and appropriateness of his possible responses to life—humour, analytic detachment, love, sorrow, *saeva indignatio*, humility; (ii) the range and depth of his understanding of himself and other men and women. This is not the same thing as sympathy: it is the parent quality from which sympathy can spring; (iii) his capacity for what might be called "unexcited joy"—by which is meant the sort of happiness which does not depend upon nervous excitement, for there is always something imposed and external in such happiness as that; (iv) his ability to be involved in and with the whole of created existence, not seeking at last to be detached or a mere observer any longer, but, as it were, to take responsibility for the world upon himself. This to the intelligence working alone is madness. Few men touch this degree of maturity for more than occasional moments.

As a help towards growth of all these kinds, reading of great books is an incomparable stimulus. Literature is a sort of log-book of a mental and spiritual journey actually being made. The literature of an age is an expression of its hopes and fears, its intuitions about the meaning of life, its discoveries about men and women who change and depart and are never the same. Every age finds out certain things about human nature and the interestingness of living which no other age has ever discovered and which no future time will quite recapture. Far more reading aloud, by parent or teacher, of good literature—without any commentary— would do as much as any single thing to awaken powers of the mind greatly in need of awakening.

Poetry is still sometimes taught as if it were a species of versified information, knowledge in the factual sense of the word. But one of the functions of poetry and of all the arts is to make the world fresh again and able to bring experiences to us. The appeal to the outer senses is only the start. Aesthetic satisfaction is never the satisfaction of the senses—they are never satisfied—but of the reason. In coming under the influence of the arts, as of natural beauty or life itself, everyone will get his own experience or fail to get it: he cannot get someone else's experience at second-hand. The essential thing is to let books and art and music come in upon one. In some subjects, the difference between what the child learns and what he is taught is small. The difference is much greater where the arts and religion are concerned.

It is important too that children, together or alone, should have a chance of actually experiencing (and more than once) some of the most typical things in our heritage of Western music, art and literature. They should all, for example, be given a chance to listen to *The Messiah*, and to Beethoven's Fifth Symphony, and to read, at some time in childhood, books so near the core of our tradition as *Robinson Crusoe*, *The Pilgrim's Progress*, *Huckleberry Finn*, to see and hear *The Tempest* and *The Magic Flute*.

History can be one of the most powerful of educators of the imagination, but if the children can see of the past only what *is* past, they are not seeing very much at all. To learn the reality of a movement or an institution they have to feel both its organic complexity and its power: it has in other words to mean something to them in their own lives —and children may well begin to learn a good deal of the essential meaning of history by feeling for themselves that they are really Londoners, or New Yorkers or Bostonians, or members of their own village looking out at the same hills their ancestors saw a thousand years ago. What is really romantic about the men of history is that we are so startlingly like them, not that we are so different. But much depends upon the meaning and the understanding which we can share with children as we take music, literature, history, with them.

I am not, of course, saying that art and music and literature and history are subjects through which the feelings of every boy or girl can be reached or educated. For many chemistry or biology or mathematics rightly taught will bring wonder and humanity more than any of the arts could do. Even when the feelings are involved, the mere stirring of emotion is not in itself educative: the intelligence must be thoroughly exercised at the same time. But without emotion it is impossible to learn how to be human, how to be an individual and how to be really moral. For opinions and beliefs which have been arrived at without feeling are beliefs and opinions merely at second-hand. They never become really one's own.

One of the difficulties in the education of the senses and the understanding is the lack of status which sensitiveness and experiencing power still have in schools, as compared with athletics and the exercise of the mind cleverly, logically and analytically. Much may depend upon whether the pupil can catch from the teacher or a parent or a friend some inkling of how much of his personality to give to an experience. There are people who would be surprised that a work of art or a piece of music could be loved rather than merely liked or enjoyed. Some of them are in that condition because no one with whom they have been has loved any work of art. Enthusiasm is infectious, but so are degrees of awareness. If a teacher is to get the intensity of effect that makes all the difference, he must really care. A human being who is fully alive and to whom causes matter helps to make other people less dead too.

It is not only, however, that children at school—and students at universities—should have their power to experience preserved, instead of being allowed to starve or shrivel. They must be encouraged to keep the ability which all of them had nearer the beginning of their lives to convey experience to others as experience. This is in part a problem of the acquisition of a suitable language or of suitable media for its expression.

We normally learn to express in our mother tongue statements which are true to fact, descriptive statements and statements intended to cause others to share our opinions or obey our wishes. It has been pointed out[2] that in the seventeenth century the aim of all scientists was to reduce phenomena to objective terms so that they might be described in impersonal scientific language. Since then, with the increasing emphasis on science and especially technology in our civilization, the capacity to hear and understand the overtones of meaning has slowly but continuously declined. But a statement objectively "true" can still be false to the intensity of our experience. In babyhood a smile, or a snuggle, or a glance, suffices to convey feeling. In childhood, boys and girls express in their play their wonder and perplexity and thus assimilate the experiences given them by the facts of birth and marriage, suffering and death. In adult life feelings and experiences are too complex to be properly expressed without complication and symbol. It is through subtle metaphor and symbol we have to speak—whether our medium be words or paint or musical notes—if we are to be able to speak at all. A symbol is not only a means of getting into touch with truth but of getting into touch with power. Not to be able to share an experience is frustrating and inhibiting to our development of being and of freedom. It is to ask for emptiness: to diminish our capacity for absorbing the world.

It is no accidental symptom that the typical approach to the writing of compositions—whether in periods devoted to

[2] *See* Michael Roberts: *The Modern Mind*, pp. 93, 117 and 126.

history, science, geography, social studies, or, most usually, in English—emphasizes the overwhelming importance of planning the structure. Now planning is extremely important. But it is not an early part of the task of writing. Part of the difficulty of creative expression in any medium is that the conscious will may interfere too soon. There are times for passiveness and times for sustained and tense effort. Impulses must be allowed for a while to go free if we are to express the deeper parts of the mind. There is a place for free association in English and art work, for dance and mime in the physical education lesson, as there is a place for travel and day-dream in the holidays.

The first necessity for writing well is that a person should have something to say: something that he very much wants to say, some subject in which he is really interested. When this is the case there is always hope that even a comparatively dull person will be able to write something worth reading. But children—and grown-ups too—are often not aware of how interested they really are in a great number of things. They are not in touch with the stores of fact, observation and experience which have been put away into unconsciousness by their own minds. One mark of the fundamentally uneducated man is that he has lost touch with his own real ideas and feelings, and because of this seizes hold of books and the cheap press to give him emotions and opinions, however unreal and second-hand they may be. A familiar difficulty in writing is that words will not come even when we earnestly want them to do so; or, with a fluent writer, that the words which come arise from a superficial stratum of the mind. The preliminary to good writing is to find out what we have, and failure to do this is the underlying cause of many bad essays, descriptions, and stories—in a word, of much dull writing. Dull writing is bad writing: the first of crimes is dullness.

Ideas, even unexpected ideas, are crystallizations of what is already present in the mind. The process of writing is not one of a mechanical recording of sentences waiting to be recorded, but rather a bringing up into the light of day of thoughts and feelings which, but for the act of writing, would never have come into being at all. As A. Clutton-Brock, the famous essayist, says, "If I try to say something exactly, I am not trying to say what I have to say already. I am trying to make myself in saying it. When Beethoven wrote a symphony he was not writing down something which had already stamped itself on his mind, he was making himself as well as the symphony, becoming more and more precisely Beethoven as he achieved a more and more precise expression of Beethoven."

The act of expressing experiences is a creative act: it is indeed a continuation and completing of the experience itself. "How can I tell what I feel till I see what I say?" As André Gide used to ask. If a man is trying to paint he is not trying to reproduce in his painting something which is waiting complete in the mind to be reproduced; he continues the act of experiencing as he tries to convey it to the canvas. Trying to capture an experience in words or in music is a training for anybody in being real. It is part of the process of objectifying a self which in that very act comes to birth. It is an integral part of the education of feeling and of insight.

The education of power to express asks for great humanity and understanding on the part of the teacher. He has to respect not only a child's ability to create but also his inability. "A child who feels diffident and empty," says Marjorie Hourd, author of *Some Emotional Aspects of Learning*, "will soon begin to be surprised at the way he revives and finds that after all he has got something to say with a teacher who sees this emptiness as a feeling of inadequacy which can be cured by the right treatment and not as innate stupidity with which he has been forced to deal by a malign fate. Once this kind of expression is liberated the technical aspects of writing come into their own." And that is true whatever the medium of expression; it is true of miming, acting, pottery, painting, as well as writing.

More room ought to be found for the discussion in school hours of questions of value—whether in periods devoted to the arts or elsewhere. Too often the discussion of such questions does not find appropriate place anywhere in the timetable. That this should be so is a further indication that something is wrong with our understanding of what a "subject" is. In what subject, for example, is it altogether right and proper to spend half an hour in asking why it is wrong for people to tell lies? or in considering the nature and manifestations in ordinary life of the workings of self-interest? or in talking about family and personal relationships?

But the wider and deeper we see the scope of education to be, the more subtle the process appears. Learning to judge human character, learning how to sum up a situation, learning how to make friends—all are aspects of education. Only part of the education given by any school comes from the study of a particular set of subjects. Only part of any education is the product of deliberate and controlled arrangement. Much of the education of understanding will certainly take place out of the classroom altogether —a good deal of it, one hopes, in the home, and some of it in Sunday School or church.

8

RELIGION AND EDUCATION TODAY

1

Though much evidence could be marshalled to show that
our age is not an age of religious faith and that our society
is apathetic about religious observance, there is evidence too
that the Western world is not easy about this state of affairs. In England, the Education Act of 1944 shows the
national conscience at work in a curious way: by it the
schools are trusted, as it were, to keep a core of religion
alive within the nation's children even if the parents in
large proportion are detached from the churches and give
little religious teaching in the home. The explanation, at
any rate in part, is that though a belief in religion is not
actual in the majority of people, many of them wish it were.
They would like to be able to acknowledge a greater faith
than a modern outlook and the findings of science will, they

feel, permit. Religious belief is recessive in them rather than dominant.

In America, though religious instruction is prohibited in the public schools, there are many signs that national concern about the loss of spiritual *raison d'être* is growing. It is increasingly acknowledged as the strength of many independent and parochial schools (whatever their weaknesses) that they are on a religious foundation. There is a nation-wide effort to urge the teaching of "moral values"— for America is shy of the adjective "spiritual" and, not without cause, fearful of differences between sects. And the majority of Americans—well over sixty per cent of the whole nation—are churchgoers again.

It would indeed be very surprising if in the twentieth century belief had ceased to exist. For almost the whole of the human race, as far back as records can take us, has lived religiously—a cogent proof of the relevance and importance of religion. Religion has been one of the great welling sources of our culture, the energizer of many of the currents still flowing within it, the creator of much of its pattern of values. Western civilization is not materialist in its origin and inspiration: it could never have come into existence without a belief that was absolute and passionate in the value of the individual human spirit.

It is still profoundly true to the actual experience of every man and woman that life has much mystery within it and about it; indeed that in almost all important and significant moments of our life we are involved in mysteries rather than in problems.[1] Man is not to be explained simply in terms of bodily or mental function; birth and

[1] Cf. Marcel: *Being and Having*, p. 113.

death are instinct with a wonder for him which cannot be destroyed or cancelled out by a demonstration that they are merely natural and physical processes and that that is their total meaning. The material world is, as it were, the communicating medium between human spirits which are, partly at any rate, outside it. Even in these days of apparent unbelief, the believer will discover that his influence is one that finds a home in the hearts and minds of many of his contemporaries and fellows, his own children and his pupils—even though they may not be able to accept the beliefs intellectually and right up to the conscious level. He may, to adapt Sir Walter Moberly's words, "put forward opinions which are novel, in the sense that the majority of us did not previously know that we held them, or policies which we did not previously know we intended. Yet we did hold them or intend them, in that, when they are propounded, we recognize, accept and acclaim them. They come to us, not as strange and alien, but as a revelation of the deepest truth of our own minds, though we could never have articulated them for ourselves . . . They explain us to ourselves." [2]

Some sort of philosophy of living, however unconscious, everyone must have. The choice is not really between any or none, but between philosophies which reckon with more of the facts and experiences which life gives us or with fewer. If men are brought up to believe that cut-throat competition is right as a principle, that "devil take the hindmost" is an expression of the ultimate law on which the universe is built, they are not likely to think in terms of Christian civilization. An intense faith in the inevitability

[2] *The Crisis in the University*, pp. 141-2.

of "progress" will in the long run produce a people whose moral as well as whose economic conduct is one of *laissez faire*.

If he is conscious of possessing beliefs, why should not a man honestly affirm that he does in fact hold them, and beliefs which certainly cannot be wholly defined in intellectual terms? But essential humanity and a faith that there is meaning in the universe go together—even though that faith can never be proved. If belief be only opinion it does not, of course, much matter at all. As William Temple once remarked, if when a man says that he believes in God he means that he is inclined to suppose that there probably exists a Being who may not inappropriately be called God, then it certainly does not much matter whether he believes or not. But real belief is not the product or outcome of a logical argument regarding probabilities. No one can persuade us into appreciating the beauty of mountains or sky or sea if we do not feel it for ourselves. It is because of some inward recognition and acknowledgment that we believe, when we see them, in courage and goodness, in humility and self-sacrifice, and in suffering so borne that it creates instead of destroys. One cannot help having faith in these things; one knows intuitively that they have value and truth and meaning. But to a detached scepticism the courage and goodness and self-sacrifice of men are, ultimately, interesting irrelevancies; since there are no such things as ultimate values, they can, however much we may regret the fact, have no more than a passing significance.

The truth of a religion is proved indeed not by textual criticism or dogmatic subtleties, but by that truth to human nature which the deep experiences of men find in it.

Christianity is not a series of doctrines somehow captured and held at all costs. It is a series of beliefs *in*, not a series of beliefs *that*. Its secret lies in its approach to life; for the first of Christian virtues, the one on which all the others are built, is humility, and the primary Christian quest is not power or pleasure but an understanding of God and one's fellowmen. So too with Judaism and some other of the world's great religions. It is a fallacy to suppose that discoveries about life can be made from the outside, that explanations can strip the veil of mystery from the world and that remedies which are external can cure all human ills.

Religious education, in essential, is an education of attitude and awareness, an indoctrination though with the permission of the reason, a turning of the soul to light. To think of it more superficially is to deceive oneself about its nature.

2

What are the fundamental realizations we want our children to come to as a consequence of their religious education, whether that education be given in the home—as much of the deepest religious education has always been—or in the church or the school?

First, I suggest, we want to help the growing boy and girl to realize the "givenness" of the universe. Though science can study facts and formulate laws, and though its application can help to make life more comfortable, in the last resort it can do nothing to change the nature of things.

Man is mortal: there is a loneliness about him that is inescapable.

Secondly, we want him to realize that standards are ultimately not man-made. This is, for most people to whom it comes, a slow realization. We cannot speed its growth any more than we can speed the growth of a frog by cutting off a tadpole's tail. There is moral as well as material pattern and principle in the universe; otherwise forgiveness and love would have no meaning. Teachers and children alike are beings prone to sin—that is, they run athwart the pattern—and are the same in their need for an absolute sort of salvation which no human agency conceivably can give. It is simply not facing the facts to imagine a material and self-absorbed happiness to be the main goal of human life. Life is too important for that. And to fit the mind only for living a happy life in the body may be to unfit it for a life far more worth while. Cordelia can hardly be said to have lived a happy life, nor Sir Thomas More, nor Jesus himself.

Thirdly, we want them to realize the validity of the knowledge brought to them by sympathy and insight, and indeed the non-validity in many fields of merely factual knowledge or knowledge brought in by the reasoning powers alone.

The most natural place for the early religious education of the child is the home, because it is there that the community (as personified by the mother and the father) are most naturally and intimately in touch with the child's real life. Much of this religious education will quite inevitably be caught and absorbed; some of it will be taught. Religious education always starts from membership of a group which has a religious outlook, even if the group consists of only two people: a parent and his child, a teacher and a pupil. Only when such an orientation has been given does religious instruction become possible. For without it the facts retailed in religious instruction will bear a quite different meaning or be meaningless. An attitude of belief must be present before beliefs can be taught. But whatever a child's home life and earliest religious education may have been like, it remains true that he is not likely to discover what Christianity or any other great religion is about save through a personal and intimate challenge. "All real life is meeting." It is the level at which the meeting takes place that makes it more real or less real.

Ideally the church, as a society of people who come together week by week with the common purpose of worshipping God and meditating upon His word, should be the place in which many discoveries are made in the field of personal relationships. For in its fellowship and community people ought to be able to meet each other as real persons instead of, as so often elsewhere, functionaries or rivals or on some other superficial level.

In Christian schools where religious instruction is part of the curriculum children should no doubt come to learn about the Old Testament and what the prophets had to say whose books are parts of it; about Christ and His conception of God; about the doings of St. Paul and many more recent missionaries; about the history of the Church and the formulation of doctrine which it has made. And in Jewish schools, too, the teachings of the Scriptures, the study of the succession of prophets and preachers down to modern times, the work of the synagogue, will form the basis of what is taught. But it remains true, both in Christian circles and Jewish, that the teaching of these matters is not the fundamental thing. The only basis upon which religious instruction can be given, if it is to be religious and not in reality secular, is that of a living feeling and perception of the nature of religion caught from someone else or from a group. First must come the turning of the heart in the right direction; only after that can religious knowledge be taught. Religious faith is a series of discoveries made as a consequence of taking up a point of view. The long-term test of good Scripture teaching is not only that one should know the main content of the Bible, not even that one should have been encouraged to go on reading it for oneself when schooldays are left behind, but that one should get a personal apprehension of meaning from it when one does.

The mere teaching of religious history and discussion of religious problems cannot do more than a little for the religious education of children. Even the devils in Milton's pandemonium discussed religious subjects. It does not need any personal belief in the truth of what one is talking about for one to be able to teach it in some sense of the word teach. The teaching of religious history and doctrine in a thoroughly detached way is indeed justifiable: at least it will show one's pupils that religious history is considered important enough to be in the time-table; and that some of it is quite interesting and human. Such teaching will add to the range of their concepts and of their vocabulary, even though they may have rather vague notions about what such words as idolatry, sacrifice, sin, holy, worship, spirit, really mean. For they may well come to school in these days from homes and an environment in general where the very concept of holiness is unknown; an environment in which one can be found out, or found guilty, or even commit a crime, but in which it is not possible to sin.

Nevertheless detached teaching *about* religion and about happenings to far-off folk years ago and their various religious practices is not likely to enter very deeply into them or to provide much of a religious education. Showing them pictures (or film strips, if one wants to be up-to-date) of Jesus and his disciples in their curious dresses or getting them to build models of flat-roofed Palestinian houses is not likely to do more than a little to help. Religious education properly so called must have more dimensions than the dimension of factual information only. For religion has to do with boys and girls, men and women, very much like ourselves in all essentials, even though they may have lived long ago and worn curious dresses. Religious education is learning to understand that sacrifice and idolatry and sin are as much parts of the personal lives of people today as ever and parts of the personal lives of one's teacher, one's parents, one's own self.

Yet even when taught by a believer, and taught interestingly and sincerely, Scripture may yet carry with it little awakening power, little challenge, no contribution to the being of those who hear with their ears what is taught. There will be no communication of a sense of the numinous, unless the mother or father, the priest or minister, or the teachers, whoever they may be, possess it themselves at occasional moments as they teach. There is an element of revelation in such teaching, the passing on of a mystery.

No doubt one of the reasons for the lack of interest in Christianity today is the fact that many people have never had any clear presentation made to them of what it stands for or of what Christians really believe. C. S. Lewis remarks that if we had noticed that the young men of the present day found it harder and harder to get the right answer to sums, we should consider that this had been adequately explained when we discovered that schools had for some years ceased to teach arithmetic. After that discovery we should turn a deaf ear to people who offered explanations of a vaguer and larger kind—people who said that the influence of Einstein had sapped the ancestral belief in fixed numerical relations, or that gangster films had undermined the desire to get right answers, or that the evolution of consciousness was now entering on its post-arithmetical phase.

But doctrinal teaching is only teaching about a *part* of religion, nevertheless. It is the upper part of the iceberg rather than the part below the water-level. The feeling life is more fundamental and indispensable than the life of abstract and conscious thought. To believe in God is not the same thing as being convinced that you ought to believe in Him. There is an element of personal revelation in all religion, and the prime need is that we should teach so that both heart and mind can listen. "He that hath ears to hear let him hear."

I would not suggest that the school will always or even normally (especially where the situation is one of neutrality towards religion as in American public schools) be able to give religious education in this sense: far more usually it will come through home or church or intimate friends. But at least the head of a school may do something to create a community in which religious education in the proper sense will not be impossible, and many a teacher, if his own spirit be alive, may do something to make such understanding as natural as seeing the light of day. The first element in religious education is a taking for granted that God exists. The second is a facing, without distaste or illusion, of the fact that there is a mystery about human life and that it is natural and right that men should feel, as prophets and saints and religious teachers down the ages have felt, their dependence and their incompleteness. The third element is the ethical one: a working out of the consequences for men, both in Biblical times and today, of religious conviction. All the fundamental problems in religious education today are the problems of communicating these three elements.

9

THE RELEASE OF LEADERSHIP

1

If a nation is to live with any depth in an age when temptations to superficiality abound and when the mass control of opinion is easy, there must be a constant flow into it of people whose faith in things of the spirit has been profoundly learned. There will be a need for many who not merely recognize quality when they find it in others but are able in appropriate situations to act as leaders themselves.

Every society is aware at times of its need for leadership. But "leader" is a vague term which conceals within itself a wide variety of leaders at many levels. At any moment within a complex society many kinds of leadership will be necessary for the many groups and sub-groups within it; different people may take the lead of the same group at different times or in a rapidly evolving situation.

A mother is a leader of a family in a different sense from a father; an Archbishop of Canterbury is a leader of a nation in a different sense from a Prime Minister; even a bus driver in efficient charge of his bus has to act as its captain on occasion and get the moral support of the majority of his passengers against a minority. But if anyone at all is to lead he must be accepted, at any rate for the time being, by those he leads. They must recognize in him—whether they do it consciously or, as is more probable, unconsciously—some quality or qualities of which they and their group stand in need.

In the first chapter of this book we pointed to our need for new vision and sense of purpose, that is, for leaders who had intelligence, roots deep within the culture of the West, and a springing insight. What ground has been covered in the intervening chapters? We have argued that men are inevitably conditioned in great degree by the society in which they are brought up and the temper of the age to which they belong. Different parts of the same society, however, may be differently tempered; some may emphasize recessive rather than dominant elements in the society as a whole and point to different futures for mankind. In our own time, the widespread search of Western man is for happiness, wealth, knowledge and power. Men are taught many technical skills and are becoming increasingly efficient in arranging material things so that life can be made—if war does not overwhelm them—more orderly and more comfortable for almost everybody. And the education they are given tends to fit them more and more for progress of this kind.

But clever though men may be in discovering the ways

in which nature works and harnessing her to their service, ingenious though their new tools are, of a thousand kinds, complex and certain though the process of living an interesting existence may be made for everyone—human life at this level is, all said and done, an escape. It is an escape further into the prison, however interesting its walls and however well concealed the fact that the echoes we make in its passages are but echoes. There can be little reason and small importance in an existence like this.

The way to freedom, the only way, is not by trying to escape, but by learning to live at a deeper level. To do this means learning truths and traditions that are today recessive rather than dominant. The education needed will in the first place be an education unconsciously absorbed, in the home and among friends, in school and in university communities which know the values for which they stand, which have a belief in the things of the spirit, which can foster passivity and willingness to listen as well as activity and the power to think in a straight line. "Indoctrination" is thus involved; but there must also be, for any who are to learn to be leaders, battles within the conscience, discipline, loneliness and struggle. There is nothing but a superficial freedom—deceptive and heartless—to be found without an acceptance of responsibility, a personal commitment which is at bottom an expression of personal responsibility for controlling, as far as may be within one's limited power, the direction in which one's civilization shall take its next steps. The leadership we need is the leadership of men in whom material values are subordinate to others.

Yet the release of leadership of high potential can hardly

occur unless there are many people who will acknowledge
it as leadership. It is by no accident that the periods when
England has produced great composers have been periods
when many people have been interested in singing, in
music making and in music. Horace Mann would hardly
have been permitted to take the lead in so thorough-going
a way as Secretary of the Massachusetts School Board
between 1837 and 1849 had he lived forty years earlier or
forty years later. Some possible leaders have been put to
death and many more have been made ineffective by other
means because their community did not recognize them as
having right on their side. Potentiality for leadership can
only become actual if a group authorizes and allows. Permission to lead will be given only if the group perceives
and approves, in however shadowy a fashion, something
of the general direction in which it is going to be led by
the leader it acknowledges. There is certainly a relationship
between the kind of leaders a society gets and the kind it
deserves. The problem once again is a problem of communication: just as people can only really hear what is
said if it is spoken in a language they know, so they will
only really be prepared to hear the truth if they have faith
that they are going to be told the truth and not lies. It is
in fact only possible to tell truths to a company which will
go halfway towards understanding what is meant.

It follows, first, that for the release of one leader of high
potential we need a number of people almost ready to go
in the direction he wishes to take. To educate for leadership is not a matter of educating the leader only. It follows,
second, that those who are to lead a nation or a group must
be really members of it; they must be men who have a

stake in the community they are going to lead. The quality of their leadership is likely to depend upon the centrality and representativeness of their membership in their community as much as upon the profundity or originality of their minds. Indeed too much originality may be fatal to their being granted authority as guides and pioneers. A leader who is going to matter deeply to a society must start to lead it from the inside; he will help those being led to feel their own responsibility, not take that sense of responsibility from them. And so, as he leads them, men will feel that their own lives have more meaning and are more worth while. He will have power within them and not merely over them; and they will become more sure themselves that they really belong to the group.

Sheer capacity for belief is of immense importance in any community: a few people having both power to believe and a strong intelligence will have great influence. A society, or a school, in which a number of such people are living purposefully, willingly taking responsibilities upon themselves, will help all who belong to it to find real things they want to do, to become more genuine in feeling and more responsible in action. It will be a community which naturally gives birth to leaders. Our problem is to make nations of this sort—or if not nations at first, then individual homes and schools of this sort—in which powers of leadership will be released.

2

Though a home or a school cannot exist in isolation from the society surrounding it, it can certainly influence the direction in which that society is developing. It can emphasize this tendency or that within it, this half-formulated wish or that one. It can suggest that individual ambition has rights that are all but limitless or it can help self-interest to evolve into an interest much more widely conscious. It can encourage initiative and nourish intelligence or allow them to wither. The more any schools—or the teachers within them—have representativeness, humanity and vigour of mind the greater their chance of educating men with quality and purpose. There is no doubt that in the past both in England and in America some schools, colleges and universities have been far more successful than others in doing this. Among the many reasons for this I would pick out three: the degree of their acceptance by society, the "life" that has been in them, and their possession of some teachers—not necessarily any great proportion—who have been very much alive, very humane, and very representative of their society. I will annotate these three points.

(i) Schools cannot easily give their children some of the more deep and subtle kinds of confidence simply on their own. It follows that if we are to release powers of leadership in more people, to put more vision and intelligence, belief and will at the disposal of the community, we shall have not merely to trust schools and teachers more but to show them clearly that we are doing so. As things are, far too few schools are habitually thought of as belonging either to England or to America as great and whole societies and nations. People do not take any obvious pride in the majority of them and a career of teaching in them carries little status with it. This is in part because the work they are doing is so little realised. Academies like Eton and Shrewsbury, Groton and Phillips Andover, are generally known and get quite a deal of publicity: most schools exceedingly little. Schools need to take more pride, and have a much deeper confidence, in themselves.

In England, it is true that some Local Education Authorities are administering their schools, and especially their secondary schools, so that they have increasing independence. The heads of schools are allowed more scope than they were even a few years ago in choosing members of their staff. Each secondary school has its own governing body, which is allowed a considerable measure of authority. Greater powers are delegated to the governing body and the head personally in financial matters than used to be granted them. That schools should be given as much independence and as much freedom as they can responsibly take, instead of as little, is a matter of national consequence. External control must be seen as a stage on the way—however long that way may be—to control of a more inward kind. It is adolescence, not full maturity. The principle we are urging is more or less the same as that underlying the development of British colonial relationships. The Commonwealth ideal is the willing co-operation of independent units rather than the control of a single empire.

(ii) It has been suggested in some quarters that since some schools are not yet fitted for a considerable degree of independence, no schools ought to be allowed any. They should all be treated as much alike as possible, whether old or new, grammar or modern, college preparatory or vocational, and there should be no suspicion that some are more privileged, some less. I believe that there are manifold dangers in this rather mechanical understanding of what equality should mean, and a threat to life and quality. The "life" and "personality" of a good school or college are precious. And it is easier to kill than to quicken.

"There is liberty in dungeons," says Rousseau in *Emile*. In other words, it is possible to have plenty of freedom in a place where a man would not greatly mind whether he had much of it or not, and where it would be of small use to him anyway. In the same way, there is equality in being dead, but that is hardly the sort of equality for which we are looking. If we can only get more equality by deadening more people than we bring to life, it seems doubtfully worth while. If we find that our pursuit of equality is removing some incentives without substituting others, is making life less spirited—if, in other words, we find that the equality we are producing is the equality which a battery of machines would have, rather than a community of men and women—we must beware, for we are probably on the wrong track. George Orwell, in his terrible book *1984*, imagines a society made up of administrators who, for the most part, possess equality with one another—but their equality is the equality of mechanized men, men mass-produced by propaganda so that they all have the same views, cry out with joy or sorrow at the same stimuli; a society where differences of intelligence hardly matter, or differences of individual temperament either, a society in which the human spirit itself is insidiously destroyed. Hardly anyone could wish for equality of this sort or upon these terms. Equality of opportunity—for schools or individuals—does not mean that an equal number of opportunities should be given to everyone to do the same things. To offer people an equal chance of finding interest or meaning in life will involve treating them very differently. But to give them permission to be equally mechanized is to give them nothing at all. The "life" of a good school is one evidence that it is a community and not merely an institution.

(iii) But the most important thing of all in making it possible for schools to release leadership, to raise the level of response and vision in their pupils, is that there should be more teachers of high quality, men and women awake and aware, representatively civilized. At the end of the first chapter we spoke of the need for people who felt as disturbingly personal issues the conflicts that were really important in the life of their society, who fought its battles within themselves. Teachers of this magnitude can be found in any type of school and in every university. There are not enough of them, of course, and perhaps sometimes —though this is rare—their value is not recognized and they are unduly curbed and strait-jacketed because they seem too unconventional. But we could certainly do more to ensure that a greater number of men and women of this calibre entered the teaching profession. Many people do not find out that they are born teachers until after they have entered it and numbers who might have gone into it are attracted to other professions because of the freedom, the salary, the status and recognition which those professions give and which teaching, especially in a maintained school, as yet does not. How many teachers are asked to serve on representative national committees—even committees upon education itself? How many teachers ever appear in public Honours lists? How do salaries paid to teachers—especially at their top levels—compare with salaries earned in business, law, medicine or the federal service by people bearing at all comparable degrees of responsibility?

And we could certainly do more to help our teachers become more representatively cultured and civilized as the years go on, instead of succumbing to the dangers inherent in the situation at present. There is need to encourage greater mobility within the profession as between one part of the country and another, between one type of school and another, between teaching and teacher training—and all this has financial implications; there is need for many more intimate contacts between staffs of schools of varying types. The links are still far too tenuous.

There is immense scope too for universities in refreshing and stimulating the teacher. And here some great advances have been made in some areas both in England and America through the work of Schools and Institutes of Education, which can be channels through which vitalizing currents can flow in both directions between universities and schools. What is needed is not only a continued addition of new knowledge but continued incentives to think and feel anew: to keep sensibility and imagination awake and to work out a personal philosophy of life and education.

3

The philosophy of life and of education which we hold matters to what we are and therefore to what we teach, whether as parents or educators professionally employed.

If we are animals in essence, "animals behaved in by our instincts," then the appropriate task for education would seem that of educating for as much happiness as is compatible with some happiness for other people. And if, as seems likely, men are really happier when half-awake, they ought to be kept half-awake—thinking about nothing in general—rather than roused to see their own misery. But if we are not irredeemably animal, the aim of education must be to help the young to grow into persons able to rise to experiences and to deeds which express freedom and inward spirit and therefore have authority. What indeed is any authority at last but the expression of inward spirit recognized by other spirits? The final task of education is not one of addition only—the addition of knowledge or manners or happiness or even experiences; rather, it is a task of revelation and thus of transformation. It is comparatively easy to add technical accomplishments to men and women: even a technique of humility can be acquired without too much expense of effort, particularly if one starts young enough. But real humility costs much more: and the exercise and expense are of both heart and mind.

The ability at moments to be thus free demands roots which go down into a spiritual heritage. It means so experiencing and suffering that one has come to belong to the past as well as the present. No one can control change simply by making changes: it takes principles, a sense of values and a personal will to bring about changes that are significant. The individual human being is the one means by which values can be brought into the world alive. If education causes men to lose touch with their own spirits it betrays its own purpose: man educated must be man intensified. But that does not mean that he is not still human. He can never without danger forget for long his own mortality in the body. At the last he will be content:

> "If his temporal reversion nourish
>   (Not too far from the yew tree)
> The life of significant soil."

BIBLIOGRAPHY

Allen, Edgar Leonard. *Existentialism from Within.* New York: The Macmillan Co., 1953.

Benedict, Ruth. *Patterns of Culture.* Boston: Houghton, Mifflin Co., 1934.

Butler, Samuel. *Erewhon.* New York: E. P. Dutton & Co., Inc., 1910.

Clutton-Brock, Arthur. *The Necessity of Art.* New York: George H. Doran Co., 1924.

Coburn, Kathleen, editor. *Inquiring Spirit.* New York: Pantheon Books, Inc., 1951.

Coleridge, Samuel Taylor. *Table Talk,* arranged and edited by T. Ashe. New York: Harcourt, Brace & Co., 1923.

Council for Curriculum Reform. *The Content of Education.* London: University of London Press, 1945.

Dawson, Christopher. *Understanding Europe.* London: Sheed & Ward, Ltd., 1952.

Eliot, Thomas Stearns. *The Cocktail Party*. New York: Harcourt, Brace & Co., 1950.

—— *The Family Reunion*. New York: Harcourt, Brace & Co., 1939.

—— "Four Quartets," from *Complete Poems and Plays*, New York: Harcourt, Brace & Co., 1952.

Fromm, Erich. *Man for Himself*. New York: Rinehart & Company, Inc., 1947.

Harding, D. W. *Social Psychology and Individual Values*. New York: Longmans Green & Company, Inc., 1953.

Holmes, E. G. A. *What Is and What Might Be*. London: 1912.

Hourd, Marjorie Lovegrove. *The Education of the Poetic Spirit*. London: William Heinemann Ltd., 1949.

—— *Some Emotional Aspects of Learning*. London: William Heinemann Ltd., 1952.

Hulme, Thomas Ernest. *Speculations*. New York: Harcourt, Brace & Co., 1924.

Humby, Spencer Robert and James, E. J. F. *Science and Education*. New York: The Macmillan Co., 1942.

Itard, Jean Marc Gaspard. *The Wild Boy of Aveyron*, translated by George and Muriel Humphrey. New York: Century Company, 1932.

Jaspers, Karl. *Man in the Modern Age*. New York: Henry Holt & Co., Inc., 1933.

—— *The Perennial Scope of Philosophy*. New York: Philosophical Library, Inc., 1949.

Kilpatrick, William Heard. *Philosophy of Education*. New York: The Macmillan Co., 1951.

Langer, Suzanne Katherina. *Philosophy in a New Key*. Cambridge: Harvard University Press, 1942. New York: Mentor Edition, The New American Library of World Literature, Inc., 1948.

Lewis, Clive Staples. *The Abolition of Man.* Oxford: The Oxford University Press, 1943.

Linton, Ralph. *The Cultural Background of Personality.* New York: Appleton-Century-Crofts, Inc., 1945.

Mannheim, Karl. *Ideology and Utopia.* New York: Harcourt, Brace & Co., 1936.

—— *Diagnosis of Our Time.* New York: Oxford University Press, 1944.

Marcel, Gabriel. *Being and Having.* Boston: Beacon Press, 1951.

—— *The Mystery of Being,* 2 volumes. Chicago: Henry Regnery Co., 1951.

Mead, Margaret. *Growing Up in New Guinea.* New York: William Morrow and Company, 1930. New York: Mentor Edition, The New American Library of World Literature, 1953.

Moberly, Sir Walter Hamilton. *The Crisis in the University.* New York: The Macmillan Co., 1950.

Niblett, William Roy. *Essential Education.* London: The University of London Press, 1947.

Orwell, George. *Nineteen Eighty-Four.* New York: Harcourt, Brace & Co., 1949.

Pieper, Joseph. *Leisure, the Basis of Culture.* New York: Pantheon Books, Inc., 1952.

Plant, James Stuart. *Personality and the Cultural Pattern.* New York: The Commonwealth Fund, 1937.

Polanyi, Michael. *Science, Faith and Society.* New York: Oxford University Press, 1947.

Roberts, Michael. *The Modern Mind.* New York: The Macmillan Co., 1937.

—— *The Recovery of the West.* Toronto: Ryerson Press, 1941.

Santayana, George. *Persons and Places.* New York: Charles Scribner's Sons, 1944.

Spence, Sir J. *The Purpose of the Family*. London: 1946.

Toynbee, Arnold. *The Study of History*, abridged by D. C. Somervell. New York: Oxford University Press, 1947.

Wicksteed, Joseph Hartley. *The Challenge of Childhood*. London: Chapman & Hall, Ltd., 1936.

Wordsworth, William. *The Prelude* (1805), text edited by E. de Selincourt. New York: Oxford University Press, 1933.

INDEX

and reality of individual feeling,
34-36
and wider horizons, 30-32
Sports in English curriculum, 86-
87
Standards of conduct, 28-29

Teachers, and curriculum, 89
Teaching, close contact in, 72-73
competition and rivalry, 76-77
consciousness of self and will
power, 79-81
at deeper levels, 75-76
discipline in, 72-75
getting pupils to want things, 78-
79
relationships within group and
between groups, 77-78
responsibility, 81
self-unity, 82
See also School
Temple, William, 122
Thomas, Dylan, 109
Tradition, acceptance of, 51-53
authority of, 15-17
effect of, on character building,
20-21
in development of skills by
children, 13-14

on education, 9
on school curriculum, 20
individual freedom within, 49-
51
process of absorbing, 41-46
responsibility within, 53-56
Traherne, Thomas, poem, *Dumbness*, quoted, 2

Understanding, teaching, 103-116
ability to convey experience, 112-
116
imagination and feeling, 107-112
values, developing sense of, 103-
107
Undset, Sigrid, *The Longest Years*,
109
Uttley, Alison, *The Country Child*,
109

Values, teaching, 103-107
Vitality of pupil, maintaining, 91-92

Wicksteed, Joseph, quoted, 73
Will, development of, 80-81
Wordsworth, William, quoted, 74,
76
Writing, teaching, 113-116
Wykeham, William of, 86